No Room For The Inn

Cycle A Sermons for Advent, Christmas, and Epiphany Based on Gospel Texts

Frank Ramirez

CSS Publishing Company, Inc.
Lima, Ohio

NO ROOM FOR THE INN

FIRST EDITION
Copyright © 2022
by CSS Publishing Co., Inc.

Library of Congress Cataloging-in-Publication Data:

Names: Ramirez, Frank, 1954- author.
Title: No room for the inn : 2022-2023 Cycle A sermons for Advent,
    Christmas, and Epiphany based on the gospel texts / Frank Ramirez.
Description: Lima : CSS Publishing Company, Inc., 2022. | Includes
    bibliographical references.
Identifiers: LCCN 2022012918 (print) | LCCN 2022012919 (ebook) | ISBN
    9780788030482 (paperback) | ISBN 9780788030499 (adobe pdf)
Subjects: LCSH: Advent sermons. | Christmas sermons. | Epiphany--Sermons. |
    Bible. Gospels--Sermons. | Common lectionary (1992). Year A.
Classification: LCC BV4254.5 .R36 2022 (print) | LCC BV4254.5 (ebook) |
    DDC 252/.612--dc23/eng/20220608
LC record available at https://lccn.loc.gov/2022012918
LC ebook record available at https://lccn.loc.gov/2022012919

For more information about CSS Publishing Company resources, visit our website at www.csspub.com, email us at csr@csspub.com, or call (800) 241-4056.

e-book:
ISBN-13: 978-0-7880-3049-9
ISBN-10: 0-7880-3049-3

ISBN-13: 978-0-7880-3052-2
ISBN-10: 0-7880-3048-5

Contents

Introduction

Partway through the Sermon on the Mount Jesus said, "If your right eye causes you to sin, tear it out and throw it away... (Matthew 5:29)." I'm sure most of us who fill a pulpit have made it clear over the years that this is metaphorical language. Don't actually tear out your right eye, your right hand, or any other members of your body.

In the same spirit, I want to make it clear that I don't want you to throw our your Nativity set after preaching these Advent and Christmas sermons. Don't throw out the Christmas cards you bought on sale December 26 last year, either. Don't lead the church in some radical cleansing of Nativity symbols. We've always known some elements of the traditional Christmas pageant, like the Magi showing up right behind the shepherds instead of a year or two later, aren't quite accurate anyway.

Having made that clear, The reason I titled this book "No Room *For* the Inn" instead of "No Room *In* the Inn" is because the language behind Luke 2:7 makes it pretty clear that Jesus wasn't born in a barn because the Bethlehem Motel 6 was full. There's no room for an inn because the inn as we picture it doesn't figure at all in Luke's gospel.

And don't forget, you could get in real trouble messing with people's preconceived notions about their favorite holiday. I *should* warn you that in 1584, Francisco Sánchez de las Brozas, a professor of philology in Spain, was turned in to the Spanish Inquisition by his students for the heretical crime of criticizing the depictions of the nativity in church paintings. He insisted that the language of Luke 2:7 was very clear. The Greek word *kataluma* should not be translated "inn." It really refers to the upper room (a guest room, or family room built to accommodate extra company or growing families) set aside for Joseph and Mary on the roof of his family's home in Bethlehem. That room wasn't big enough when she went into labor, what with midwives and the need to walk her around, so she was brought down the stairs, or helped down the ladder, to the main floor where, typically, a single-story village house included space for the animals, along with the manger than held their food. The article that inspired more research is listed in the bibliography, along with a few more resources.

There's more, but even though you'll be preaching the truth that will set you free, please don't make changes in your church's Christmas Pageant, decorations, Nativity set, preprinted bulletin covers, or the Christmas cards you were planning to send out. There's value in the way we've told this story our whole lives, and besides, you don't want to risk the Spanish Inquisition.

Between the four Sundays of Advent, three Propers of the Nativity, and extra services for New Year's Day, Epiphany, and the Transfiguration, which don't always fall on Sundays, there are some extra services you may not use. Nor, thanks to the vagaries of the calendar, does Epiphany season always include nine Sundays. Therefore I encourage you, if you encounter a sermon that doesn't appeal to you, pick another from among these extras.

Much of the Epiphany season is spent with the Sermon on the Mount. To be honest, after forty years of pastoral ministry I found myself struggling to say more than "Go thou and do likewise." My interest in the this famous sermon by Jesus was rekindled a few months into the pandemic through a northern Indiana Church of the Brethren Pastor's Conference headed up on Zoom by my friend Dr. Steven Schweitzer, Academic Dean and Professor at Bethany Theological Seminary in Richmond, Indiana. Steve is a great preacher, teacher, writer, and inspired leader of Bible studies. Following his five-hour conference, from which I took copious notes, I did some more reading on my own. A few of the books are listed in the bibliography. In addition, I drew upon some of the material I wrote for the 2019 Advent devotional *Ready* (Brethren Press) and before that the 2001 Advent Devotional *Partners in Prayer* (Christian Board of Publication) as well as the book *The Christmas Star* (CSS, 2002).

We all have different denominational backgrounds. I belong to a relatively small but storied denomination, the Church of the Brethren. We had no official name prior to 1908. Before that we were known variously as the German Baptist Brethren, New Baptists, and the Dunkers. The latter was a nickname based on our mode of baptism, full immersion three times forward. Prior to 1910, we were basically one of the Plain Peoples of Pennsylvania. In referring to Brethren stories, I have taken to referring to us as the Dunkers to make the stories more serviceable.

If you are a regular subscriber to the lectionary tools provided by CSS, a few of the stories and illustrations used in these sermons may be familiar. That's because I regularly write for those elements of the SermonSuite resources known as Emphasis, Charting the Course, and StoryShare. It's a joy to be a part of this shared ministry, teaching, preaching, and learning from each other, and trust me, I use the materials I write in the sermons I preach.

Many of us in pastoral ministry don't use art often enough in our sermons. I'm one of those pastors, and in recent years I've tried to use more art in worship. Over the centuries, art has served as a Bible for Christians who may not have had reading skills. In addition, good biblical art is a great focus for devotion and prayer. For those sermons concerned with Matthew 5-7, I suggest you go online and use your search engine to find the painting "The Sermon on the Mount," by Jan Brueghel the Elder, at the J. Paul Getty Museum website. The painting is labeled "No copyright." During the sermons I will reference portions of the painting for focus and reflection. Hopefully you have the ability to project these scenes from a computer onto a screen. Make sure you can zoom in and out on various portions of the image.

I first encountered this painting on a trip to Los Angeles. My wife Jennie and I decided to play hooky from church on Sunday morning and went to the Getty where we enjoyed the many biblical scenes portrayed by classic artists over the centuries. This painting is extremely striking. It is small, 10 ½ by 12 ½ inches, but the faces of over a hundred different people are depicted in exquisite detail! If you can't access or display this painting just alter the sermons, removing any references. (And if you decide to see it in person, the painting is on display at The Getty Center, not the Getty Villa. Always check website for timed entry passes.)

Finally, you will notice that on rare occasions, as in the opening of the sermon for the First Sunday of Advent, I tell a personal story. I don't expect you to pretend you went to elementary school in Azusa, California. I hope you will read the story, and consider whether there is an analogous experience in your life.

For many of us revisiting Advent and Christmas, as well the Sermon on the Mount, can be a source of dread because we revisit these scriptures regularly. My prayer is that we will be able to approach this special time in the life of the church with excitement and joy.

The Lord bless you and keep you. I remain
Christ's servant and yours,

Frank Ramirez

Bibliography

Argyle, A.W., *The Gospel According to Matthew,* Cambridge University Press, 1963.

Betz, Hans Deiter, *The Sermon on the Mount: A Commentary on the Sermon on the Mount,* Hermeneia, Fortress Press, 1995.

Carlson, Stephen, "The Accommodations of Joseph and Mary in Bethlehem: *Kataluma* in Luke 2:7," *New Testament Studies* 56 (2010).

Hagner, Donald A., *Matthew 1-13,* Word Biblical Commentary, v. 33A, Thomas Nelson Inc., 1993.

Levine, Amy-Jill, and Ben Witherington III, *The Gospel of Luke: New Cambridge Bible Commentary,* Westminster, 2018.

Nolland, John, *Luke 1:1-9:20,* Word Biblical Commentary, v. 35A, Thomas Nelson Inc., 1989.

Milgrom, Jacob, *Leviticus 17-22: A New Translation with Introduction and Commentary.* The Anchor Yale Bible. Yale University Press, 2000.

Ramirez, Frank, *The Christmas Star,* CSS Publishing Company, 2002.

------------------, *Partners in Prayer: Advent 2001,* Christian Board of Publication, 2001.

------------------, *Ready: Devotions for Advent Through Epiphany,* Brethren Press, 2019.

To Jack Francisco Hamlyn Ramirez, my Grand-grandson. A chip off several blocks, and one blockhead — me! With three of your four grandparents having been pastors, and the other grandma more than willing to sermonize as needed, you've heard more than your share of sermons! Here are a few more.

Last Things First

I was given my first library card for the grown-up section of the Azusa (California) Public Library when I was in the fourth grade. It was a special moment. I felt like I'd read everything in the kids half of the library and I chafed to read new books. Holding my card out like a passport, I walked tentatively into the grownup section fearful I would be challenged, but I had my card in hand, just in case.

But the doors opened. I entered. A new world beckoned.

The first book I checked out that day was the novel *Second Foundation* by Isaac Asimov. I still remember the orange, pebbly library binding of that book. Cracking open the cover, I read the synopsis and learned the Galactic Empire was falling, and only Hari Seldon's mathematics could prevent thirty thousand years of anarchy and chart a course toward a new, more perfect empire.

I soon realized this was the final book of a trilogy. No matter. Reading the last book first, discovering the secret location of the Second Foundation, didn't spoil the first two books when I finally found them years later in that pre-Amazon era.

The same thing happened to me with the Nero Wolfe mysteries by Rex Stout. While serving my first pastorate in the '80s I watched a TV series based on Nero Wolfe. Though it was cancelled after only a few episodes it inspired me to check out the Nero Wolfe mystery "A Family Affair." You guessed it. With 33 novels and 41 novellas to choose from, I picked the very last one in the series, where — no spoilers here — I learned something crucial about one of the main characters.

It didn't matter. I hunted down and devoured all the books and stories. I couldn't read them fast enough.

I mention this because in Advent we do something equally counterintuitive. We tell the end of the story before the beginning. We describe the return of Jesus before we get around to telling the story of his birth. Advent is the season in the church calendar where we prepare for the coming of the Christ child, but in this scripture, as in the other lectionary years, our concern is first with the signs in the skies and the earth, and the coming of the Son of Man in glory. Only later will we talk about the child in the manger.

Yet, this doesn't spoil the story for us. If anything, knowing the glorious ending enhances our appreciation of the humble beginning.

Here's the real deal. This is how the early church learned about Jesus. The apostles proclaimed his return long before anyone got around to talking about his birth. In other words, the early church knew the ending of the story before they knew the beginning. And guess what — knowing the ending didn't spoil the story for them either.

In a way it made sense. The original proclamation of the church that Jesus was returning was more urgently important to a church under persecution than celebrating his arrival thirty years before. This was the urgent news shared by the apostles.

But as the first Christians delved into the Hebrew scriptures to learn about Jesus they discovered Isaiah pointed not only to the suffering servant, but also to a Messiah that would be a descendant of King David, who would come from Bethlehem, be born of a virgin, and come to be known as Wonderful Counselor, Almighty God, Everlasting Father, and Prince of Peace. The people who had walked in darkness suddenly found themselves in the great light of scripture.

The apocalyptic scriptures, like today's passage from Matthew, are an essential part of our leadup to Christmas. Advent opens with these words about the coming of the Son of Man. This image is not in the least mysterious. It's a way of saying "human being." But this Son of Man comes straight out of the book of Daniel, which was written at a crucial time in the history of the people of God. The stories of Daniel in the first six chapters recount the experiences of God's people when the Babylonians destroyed Jerusalem and the temple, and dragged away many of the political and economic elite into exile in Babylon. But these stories were not written down for centuries.

There's a great line in Psalm 137, recalling the great sadness of those who were taken away forever from their homes, their city, and their temple — "How can we sing the songs of the Lord while in a foreign land?" The stories, such as the three young men in the fiery furnace, and Daniel's refusal to bow to the great golden idol, demonstrate that it was possible to do precisely that. Daniel and the others accept their roles as civil servants, but still maintained a line between faithful and unfaithful behavior!

After Babylon was defeated by the Persians, God's people entered a new phase. The Persians sent many captive nations, like the Israelites, back to their homelands, and granted them religious freedom — as long as they paid their taxes on time! For the next few hundred years God's people thrived! But around the year 167 BC, their trust was betrayed by Antiochus IV Epiphanes, the ruler of the Seleucid empire. A few people rebelled against foreign domination, but Antiochus slaughtered and enslaved many of God's people who were making an open show of cooperation with that ruler, betraying them despite their efforts to be good citizens.

In response, the stories and lessons of Daniel were revived and included along with the apocalyptic promises that came to be so important to the early Christians — images of the Son of Man, seated next to the Ancient of Days, and descending on a cloud to restore God's people and God's kingdom. There were images of Michael the archangel, engaging in battle against the forces of darkness.

In today's passage, which takes place in Jerusalem during the final week before the crucifixion, in the rock solid great temple, one of the wonders of the world, Jesus predicted that it would all be destroyed. He drew upon images taken from Daniel 7:13:

> As I watched in the night visions,
> I saw one like a human being
>   coming with the clouds of heaven.
> And he came to the Ancient One
>   and was presented before him.

As well as from the prophets, such as Isaiah 13:10

> For the stars of the heavens and their constellations
>   will not give their light;
> the sun will be dark at its rising,
>   and the moon will not shed its light.

and 24:23:

> Then the moon will be abashed,
>   and the sun ashamed;
> for the Lord of hosts will reign
>   on Mount Zion and in Jerusalem,
> and before his elders he will manifest his glory.

to paint a picture of the end times. What should not be overlooked is while the earlier warning about Jerusalem included instructions about signs that could be understood, and should lead believers to abandon the city (as actually happened), Jesus specifically stated that wars and rumors of war were *not* signs of the ultimate end of the world — just the end of Jerusalem.

Those signs in the sun, moon, and stars Jesus spoke of as signs of the end times would be obvious to *everyone* when they occurred, not just a select few; as obvious as leaves on a fruit tree indicating trees would be bearing fruit. And while Jerusalem's dire destruction is something the believers should avoid at all costs, believers should take heart when it becomes obvious that the true end has come. As Jesus said "…your redemption is drawing nigh (20:28)," not your destruction.

The key thing, Jesus maintained, is to stay alert. Be on guard. Be aware.

As I said earlier, Babylon was conquered by the Persians. Afterward, some of the Jewish exiles returned to Judea. Gradually, worship was restored. The temple was rebuilt. The walls around

Jerusalem were repaired. For some centuries stability and limited self-rule returned.

Still, there was still this awkward truth, the promise made by God to King David that forever one of his descendants would reign upon the throne. There was no such king, no such country. In the second century before Jesus, the Judeans temporarily threw off their shackles and had a king for a short while, but infighting between the various factions led them to invite the Romans to help calm down the situation. The Romans didn't leave. They stayed to rule with an iron rod.

This King descended from David would be none other than Jesus, who would come again in glory, after the manner of the Son of Man's descent described in Daniel, to reign eternally. But there's also those awkward words when Jesus warned that the present generation Jesus spoke to would not pass away before these things happened. If Jesus was talking about the true end times that would lead to his return, then he was wrong. That's an uncomfortable thought. The Christian writer C.S. Lewis said that this error, if error it was, demonstrated that when God dwelt among us in human form this knowledge was kept from Jesus and that he could be wrong. That's hinted about in his next statement that neither the Son nor the angels, but only the Father knows when this will happen.

But, as I said earlier, Jesus was talking about the destruction of Jerusalem that followed his death and resurrection about forty years later. The warnings about how swiftly destruction would come, as in the days of Noah, are reminiscent of what occurred in the war between the Judeans and the Romans. The images of one individual taken and one remaining are not a prophecy of the rapture but a vivid picture of Romans murdering civilians right and left.

What is significant is that Jesus warned that the Son of Man would come, like the terrors that loomed on the horizon, when no one expects. And that is the promise, and the warning, we are faced with as we start this season of Advent. This is the last installment, the episode of our favorite series, the final book that we are reading first before we read the others.

Every series, no matter how popular, comes to an end, and when it does, the approaching series finale looms, with all sorts of speculation. Will everything be tied up in a neat bow? Will everything be left in shreds and tatters? With wars and rumors of war, many people are asking, when it comes to our planet, are we approaching the series finale?

We know that when Jesus, the king descended from David, came to this earth he did not bother to eradicate worldly kings. He established the eternal kingdom of God, to be eternally established upon his return, but permanently founded in our hearts and in the church, visible through our manner of living.

In the same way the post-pandemic church is not going to restore Christendom, a time when men wore hats and women wore white gloves, but will witness to the coming reign of Jesus, be witnesses to justice, minister to the forgotten, and celebrate Christ here and now!

So in the midst of our wild, drunken parties — okay, for us it means face planting in a bowl of Chex Mix and a platter of fudge — and the cares of the ordinary world that truly weigh us down — we will proclaim that the newborn king is more than a cute baby in a manger. This is the eternal king who carries the arc of history toward salvation, justice, and peace. This is our story.

Keep in mind that the prophets warned God's people that the Day of the Lord might be a day of judgment, not a day of joy. Jesus is warning people to be always ready for trauma, and to be prepared to be faithful in difficult circumstances. Certainly in our own times, with the epidemic of mass shootings, we have seen that we never know when terror may strike, and when it does, unfairly the youngest, and the most vulnerable, can be taken from us.

The post-quarantine church is emerging in a society that is no longer Christendom. Christianity is no longer the default setting for people in our society. We are going through a time when all of society is being shaken up. It's *not* enough to tell folks in our society that Jesus saves.

It is time for us to show not just with words but by our actions, caring for our communities, lifting all up in prayer, and serving visibly in a way that is obvious to all without constantly pointing to ourselves. It is Jesus who is coming into our broken world, now as well as at the end.

As a matter of fact, we do damage to the church (but not to Jesus) when we're constantly talking about the end of the world, then making excuses when it doesn't happen, then doing it again. We give the impression we Christians are nothing but a scattering of Chicken Littles instead of a flock under the care of the Good Shepherd. Since it will be obvious when God wraps up history for real, let us be just as obvious in our loving care for the world at large. That's what those who are seeking truth are looking for.

I'm intrigued that Jesus is suggesting we are in danger from both "wild, drunken parties" as well as the "cares of ordinary life." Both have the potential to distract us from the good news. Our cares can weigh us down, to where we feel as if we cannot act, or if our actions have no effect. But one of the liberating things about knowing the ending of the story is that no matter how meaningless the present may seem at times, history has meaning and purpose. That's why what both Jesus and the prophets were predicting, the end, is good news.

In his essay, "The World's Last Night," C. S. Lewis emphasized that since Jesus made it clear that no one knows when the world might end, it is far more important to be about the work of a disciple. Even if we have simple work to do, like caring for animals, or loftier goals, like ending human trafficking, we are to be busy. Christ may come at any moment, and the work we started won't be finished! Lewis says, "No matter; you were at your post when the inspection came." Yes, there's a lot to do between now and Christmas. Still, one has to ask: Are you at your post? As John the revelator prayed, "Amen. Come, Lord Jesus" (Revelation 22:20).

Amen.

Second Sunday of Advent
Matthew 3:1-12

In Those Days: The Voice Of The Time Keeper

A second is a second is a second, right? But if you're at the big game it's amazing what a difference it makes once there's less than a minute left. Suddenly the scoreboard screams those seconds in fractions. Suddenly the clock moves maddeningly fast if you're behind and agonizingly slow if you're ahead.

But that's a product of our digital technology. Sundials, or solar clocks, in the time of Jesus measured time slowly, imperceptivity, even majestically. Complicating things further, the hours weren't the same length all year round. The first hour was sunrise and the last hour was sunset. Noon was midday. That meant the hours were much shorter in late December, and much longer in late June.

Centuries went by and the idea of the way time moves didn't change. A relatively recently discovered poem from Elizabethan times that may well have been written by Shakespeare himself makes a telling point about clocks. It's called "To The Queen."

> As the dial hand tells o'er
> The self-same hours it had before,
> Still beginning in the ending,
> Circular account still lending,
> So, most mighty Queen, we pray
> Like the dial day by day
> You may lead the seasons on...

We think of a clock dial and we think of a hand for hours, minutes, and seconds. Yet according to a scholar named Helen Hackett: "...the standard type of clock, then, was one-handed, and the dial hand would rotate slowly, moving round only one-twelfth or one-twenty-fourth of the circumference of the dial in each hour. The notion of the dial hand is therefore not, as modern readers might assume, an image of time racing on, but an image of steady slowness, of progress which is inexorable yet barely perceptible…" (*The New Oxford Shakespeare: The Complete Works*, p. 1507.)

If we want to think of time in a biblical sense, first of all we need to slow down. Then we need to go back, *way* back, to the beginning, in Genesis. On the first day God created light, but it was not until the fourth day that God created the sun and moon to measure time. That may seem strange, but the reason for this is that in most ancient religions the sun and moon were major gods. In Genesis, they were not in the least divine. They were set in the heavens so they might serve "for signs and for seasons and for days and years" (Genesis 1:14).

The rising and the setting of the sun (yes, we know it is the earth that is turning, but that's the way it looks to us mere mortals who live on the planet) mark days, while the phases of the moon correspond to months. The solar year is 365 ¼, sort of, while the lunar year is 354 days, kind of, with an extra month added to make up for the spare change of the days missed in order to make that lunar year keep time with the seasons.

While we think of time as something that can be measured precisely, sliced and diced to the tiniest fraction, for Jesus and his contemporaries time was a quality defined by light and darkness, the seasons, and the position of the sun and the stars. There was a quality to which God's people found themselves, waiting for a Messiah descended from King David to bring deliverance. When would God do this? Hard to say. After all, as it says in scripture, "with the Lord one day is like a thousand years, and a thousand years are like one day."

We try to be precise. We pick a day, March 21, or the 20 or 22 depending where exactly the earth reaches a certain point in its orbit around the sun in a particular year, and we call that the first day of spring. But really, spring can catch us by surprise, arriving early, allowing the peonies and snowdrops to emerge with startling speed! Or the grey of winter and a cover of snow can drag into April. Then, suddenly, we realize we're surrounded by glory. Despite what the calendar says, you really can't tell when a season begins. But you know it once it arrives.

Then God did something even more astounding with time in that first chapter of Genesis. As we have just said, days, months, and years can be inferred from the creation God gave us. But on the seventh day God rested, and in commanding us to follow that example God created the week.

The week is a totally arbitrary unit of time wrapped in mystery that is not related to the solar year — there's a remainder of one day if you divide 365 days by 7. It's not related to the lunar month, which is 29 ½ days and is not divisible equally by 7 either. Indeed, there have been calendar reformers who have insisted we need to ignore the week and create a logical calendar. After the French Revolution there was a move to create a logical ten-day week. Reformers have tried to get us to create a 365 day calendar, where January 1 would fall on a Sunday every year, January 2 on a Monday, and so on, then throw in an extra day every year and two extra days in leap year that are not attached to any day of the week, but people resisted. Don't mess with the Sabbath. We live by God's time.

When we live by the week, we live by God's time. God is the time keeper. God's viewpoint, whether a day is like a thousand years or vice versa, is the one that counts.

When in Matthew's gospel, John the Baptist burst upon the scene "in this day" to tell us it was time to make straight a path through the desert because the Lord's anointing was coming, he was right on time. God's time. Time was not to be measured. Time was *urgency*. We only have today. We live in the moment. We remember the past, but we can't get back to it. We foresee the future but only hazily, and without any guarantee that there will even be a future.

A thousand years ago and more, another people felt the same urgency to make straight the paths in the wilderness, and to do so without the usual tools we associate with surveying. The ancestral Puebloans who lived in what we now call the southwest

United States lived a hardscrabble life in the deserts, planting and growing corn in every spot where precious rain might fall and crops might grow, hunting the animals that shared their habitat, and living lives that were brief by our standards, 25 - 35 years, judging from the evidence that remains.

But in the sun, moon, and stars they saw the measurement of the divine. They built great buildings, not to live in, but for ceremonial purposes, aligning doors, windows, and walls with the days of the solstices and equinoxes, the measure of the seasons. They made roads in the desert, straight and true, for ceremonial processions that led to the place we now call Chaco Canyon, which was the center of the universe for many of them. Though their lives were short, they knew they were a part of something greater.

John the Baptist came out of the desert, out of the wilderness, to call the people away from the political intrigues of his time, and the frantic necessity of carving out a livelihood in tumultuous times. He came to remember Isaiah's call to make straight the roads in the wilderness, to recognize something magnificent was happening, and to prepare the way for the Lord. In Isaiah's time that road was meant to lead people back from exile to the ruins of Jerusalem and temple, that they might rebuild and restore. In John's time, the people were to recognize in the midst of their short lives that something greater was going on, and they were a part of it. They were preparing to receive the great Messiah promised in times past and eagerly anticipated in their time.

People answered the call. As we read in Matthew, rich and poor, the occupied and the military occupiers, the tax collectors and the overtaxed, religious leaders and those who felt marginalized by their faith, all of them came to the Jordan to hear this message. They didn't get a text message: "Baptismal Service, River Jordan, 10:30." They heard "Repent!" that literally meant, turn your mind around, look at the world in a different way, start walking in a different direction. It's true — repenting is not an action that happens in a moment, but with a change of orientation becomes the journey we begin in a totally different direction than before. The kingdom was near — near in the sense that is was rushing closer and closer, but also in the sense that it was already in their midst.

Like many who preach the good news, John started out with the bad news. "You brood of vipers!" he said. "Who warned you to flee from the wrath to come?" (Matthew 3:7). But if you could take this strong medicine and stay — there was hope.

And John concluded his message by pointing to the one even greater who was coming, the one he was not worry to carry his sandals for, the one who would baptize with the Holy Spirit.

When we gather together on Sunday we try to come on time. We try to start on time. Most of all, we try to end on time. The hymns, the prayers, the offerings, the sermon, should time out pretty close to what we expect every week. There are dinners in the oven that were started on timer and we don't want them to burn. There's a game on in the afternoon we intend to watch. There is laundry to be done, clothes to be folded, homework to check, and any other number of tasks.

But if we're not careful, we'll end up being ruled by time, instead of responding to the time and recognizing this is more than the season for baking cookies and sending Christmas cards. It's a time to reflect, repent, and restore our commitment to the coming kingdom of Jesus.

Good news! The king is coming! The king has come in our midst, God entering into history as Jesus. The kingdom of the Lord is drawing near. The word near means two things. It's not quite here but it's rushing toward us. And it's not only near, it *is* here! Start living by the rules of the kingdom.

This is good news that we preach, yet that's not what the world is hearing from us. What message about this season are we sharing? We know the answer to the stress and despair that accompanies what's supposed to be a season of joy. How can we communicate that? It's not a matter of whether we see the clock madly rushing down to zero at the end of the game! It's whether we're living urgently, passionately, fully, right now.

Doing something to set ourselves apart, ignoring the most recent fashions, evaluating the most recent digital devices to see if we really need them, does not mean they are evil, but that we want to evaluate if we can live according to the way of Jesus with or without them. Many people think the Amish are against technology. Not true at all. But they are always evaluating whether innovations draw families apart or bring them closer together, wary of anything that will make living less Christlike. So you will find Amish businesses that use electricity, computer, and cell phones, but their homes are still unconnected to the grid. They are setting a good example for all of us. It's not just a matter of getting out of the rat race. It's a case of not being a rat anymore.

Maybe we have something to learn from television -- because television doesn't rule our lives anymore. Oh, sure, we love to watch. But now we watch on our own terms. Once there were three networks, and they made all the shows, and we watched those shows when they were broadcast or we didn't see them at all. Missing a show might mean never seeing it — ever.

But even something as crude as VHS tape let us record television and watch it later. When we got our first video recorder I taped a lot of shows. Then something funny happened. I never watched them. Without the need to live by the network's schedule, I realized I didn't care about what they were offering anyway.

Now you can watch on your own terms, and watch lots of shows that the major networks would never make. You decide what you'll see and when you'll see it.

Life should be like that. We shouldn't march to the expectations of the world. We shouldn't judge ourselves by what the world says is important.

We can choose the kingdom of God over the kingdom of the world. We can listen to a prophet like Isaiah, Ezekiel, Jeremiah, or John the Baptist. We can be baptized with fire for the Lord.

Or we can worry if our internet is fast enough, or ask why our microwave doesn't pop popcorn fast enough. Owners of sports teams try to figure out how to speed up already fast-paced games. After previews, most movies begin cutting mercilessly to shorten films. But there are some things worth waiting for, aren't there? Not everything can be rushed, or ought to be rushed.

You don't have to wear a bonnet or drive a buggy to get out

of the rat race. You don't have to own any kind of recorder. Yes, we still have to go work, and be on time for certain kinds of appointments, but you don't have to be ruled by the clock, or act like your faith is dependent on your economic status, the car you drive, or what company you think you ought to keep.

Instead, you can leave your sheep out in the fields and approach the King of kings and Lord of lords in the manger. You can be a young teenager like Mary or an older woman like Elizabeth and say, behold the handmaid of the Lord, let it be unto me according to your word! Because we serve a God who came to earth in human form and bore a cross for our sins.

Even now the day of the Lord is rushing headlong toward fulfillment and completion "by prophet bards foretold." We need to throw our current idea of time out the window. Stop trying to measure time, and start trying to LIVE time. We aren't rushing toward disaster, nor is time standing still. We are living in the present in the kingdom.

How many of us have snuck a peek at our phones to see what time it is? Peter tells us that when the day of the Lord comes, the day of accountability and judgment, it will be like a thief in the night! This is a reference to what Jesus said about the day of the Lord! It's coming. There's no telling when. So always live like the day of the Lord is upon us, and about to burst into history.

Change your mind. Change your perspective. Because the time is up. We don't worry about time. We live in the moment, serving each other, loving each other, and praising God. We are not worried about the arrival of the day of the Lord.

We are living *in* the day of the Lord.

This is the source of our peace. It is not a peace as the world gives it. It exists alongside the dangers of the world, but it is more real than the world.

The voice of the Baptist, the voice of the prophet, the voice of Jesus gives us hope and grants us peace.

Amen.

Third Sunday of Advent
Matthew 11:2-11; Isaiah 35:1-10

Couldn't Be Easier

You're not supposed to mess with holiday traditions, but we do. A couple of years ago a shock wave ran through the Facebook community. Peanuts specials like *It's the Great Pumpkin, Charlie Brown*, and especially *A Charlie Brown Christmas* were purchased by one of those special platforms and would no longer be broadcast on network television.

Even though the days are long past when the family gathered together on broadcast night and watched those specials together — nowadays it seems like there's at least one TV in every single room — once the shows weren't available in the same manner as the old days it became one of the worst things in the world.

Once the outrage went viral a compromise was made, and the shows in question were released for public broadcast at least once during the proper season. I'd be curious to know how many people actually watched, since the ones who were most vocal probably owned a Blu-Ray, DVD, and an obsolete VHS copy, but we'll see.

Well, during the holiday season I want to preach about angels, glory to God in the highest, peace among people of good will, and away in the manger, no crib for a bed — stuff like that. But the scriptures this week feature Jesus talking about John the Baptist — and not the birth of John the Baptist from Luke 1, but jumping way ahead to when John is in prison before the daughter of Herodias asks for his head on a platter because there's nothing she'd rather have for a gift from her stepfather King Herod.

That scripture doesn't put me in any sort of holiday mood, but it does get to the heart of promise, as does another scripture from Isaiah the prophet, written centuries before, which Jesus quotes for the occasion.

So clear the stage of the cows, sheep, Magi, and shepherds, and set up a different nativity set, one that features an adult Jesus standing and talking to the crowds. Suddenly the crowd parts. Some folks who are taking care of John the Baptist in prison have come to ask Jesus, on behalf of John, "Are you the one who is to come, or are we to wait for another?"

Considering that in other places John the Baptist was the one who proclaimed "Behold the Lamb of God who comes to take away the sin of the world," this might seem like an odd question, but perhaps John had expected this promised Messiah, who he had assured the crowds would baptize with fire and the Holy Spirit, would have already turned the world upside down, established the kingdom of God, and begun his reign, his foot on the necks of the Roman authorities.

Nothing of the sort happened. I'm not sure if the question asked by John through his disciples was meant to be challenging, or just a request for information. I'm not sure how the crowd reacted. Maybe they were wondering too. Regardless, Jesus treated a question from John the Baptist as a priority, setting aside whatever he was in the process of saying, and answered politely, "Go and tell John what you see and hear; the blind receive their sight, the lame walk, the lepers are cleansed are cleansed, the deaf hear, the dead are raised, and the poor have good news brought to them."

What was packed into his answer? Well, a lot of scripture, verses of hope, and verses of challenge and promise. Jesus connected the dots, not only for John and the listeners that had assembled, but for us as well, as we too wait and wonder during this season of Advent.

His reply drew upon the passages in Isaiah that pointed, hundreds of years before, to the return of the exiles in Babylon to the promised land. Now, centuries later, these words were interpreted as pointing to the kingdom of God to come. This future deliverance was not only for the strong, the survivors, but for everyone. "Strengthen the weak hands, and make first the feeble knees," wrote Isaiah. "Say to those who are of a fearful heart, 'Be strong, do not fear! Here is your God." And that God was coming with strength to not only restore the weak, but to take "vengeance, with terrible recompense. He will come to save you" (Isaiah 35:3-4).

It was in that context that "the eyes of the blind shall be opened, and the ears of the deaf unstopped; then the lame shall leap like a deer, and the tongue of the speechless sing for joy" (Isaiah 35:5-6).

This answer could be interpreted by John to mean both "Yes!" but also "Not yet!"

For those of us who are familiar with Revelation, who have, with John the Revelator, seen the skies peeled back to reveal the saints who suffered now praising the Lamb bearing the marks of slaughter with glory and honor, who know that the wheels of God's justice are turning, and that all will be revealed, this *Yes!* still challenges us. We spoke about some of this the first Sunday of Advent. But for Jesus his purpose was not just to speak of the future, but to praise John the Baptist for his work now.

He turned to the people and told them about John. Jesus quoted Isaiah 35:5-6 and 61:1 about how God will lead the ransomed back to the promised land. This journey of return and rejoicing is a message the poor, sick, and struggling should rejoice in. This is the hope upon which our season of Advent is built.

But he also quoted Malachi 3:1: "See, I am sending my messenger to prepare the way before me, and the Lord whom you seek will suddenly come to his temple. The messenger of the covenant in whom you delight — indeed, he is coming, says the Lord of hosts."

This clearly speaks of one who goes before and prepares the way to instruct them about Jesus' identity. And then Jesus adds one of the great paradoxes of the kingdom — the greatest is the least, the least is the greatest. The last is the first, the first is the last. In talking about John, Jesus is also talking about, and inviting us, to step onto this bare stage to take part in the great drama of salvation.

Anyone who has traveled through Kansas has seen seemingly endless "amber waves of grain," and off in the distance Colorado's "purple mountain majesties" praised by Katherine

Lee Bates, a social activist, in her 1893 poem "America the Beautiful." This is like the image of "a reed shaken by the wind," used by Jesus in this passage. It would have been as familiar a sight to people not only in the holy land, but throughout Middle East in that era, as those amber waves are to us. Reeds and rushes grew profusely in rivers, and were harvested for their use in sewing, in medicine, in bedding, for thatching in houses, among many other uses. Of course Jesus is not suggesting that John the Baptist is anything at all like a reed. He is like Malachi, standing tall, true, and mysterious, coming out of the chaos of the wilderness, to call the people back to faithful living while there is still time.

No, John the Baptist was no reed shaken by the wind. He told uncomfortable truths. That's why he was in prison. He stood up to Herod Antipas. When Herod the Great died, his kingdom was divided by the Romans into four parts and assigned to various client kings. Herod Antipas, one of the surviving sons — for Herod was good at murdering his own relatives if he suspected them of plotting against him — had decided to marry Herodias, his brother Philip's wife. Herodias was more than glad to switch husbands, because she was politically ambitious, and believed the Romans were more likely to favor her new husband. Regardless of the politics behind this marriage, John the Baptist quoted from Leviticus to say this was wrong — a man was only to marry his brother's wife should that brother die and leave no heir to claim his property. Now according to one historian named Josephus, Herod and Herodias had planned this marriage long before in secret as part of their plan to advance their political fortunes. Having such a popular figure as John the Baptist denounce them in public instead of accepting the fact that celebrities live by different rules was more than inconvenient. It might turn the people against them, and that in turn might alarm the Romans who wanted more than anything else peace and quiet.

John was arrested, though as Matthew was later to note "… Herod wanted to put him to death (but) he feared the crowd, because they regarded him as a prophet" (Matthew 14:5).

Even so, Herod visited John in prison to hear what he had to say, which he found compelling, even though John condemned him. Perhaps he was so tired of false flattery that any truth, even a condemning truth, was a welcome novelty.

John told the truth. It was not always a comfortable truth. It didn't please everyone. But even Herod Antipas could not turn away, as much as what John said alarmed him. He didn't dress according to the fashion. He dressed like Elijah, like Malachi, like those prophets who meant business. He was not a reed, blowing in the wind. He was an oak, standing firm against the storm's blast.

So what are we? Reeds that shake against the wind, whatever direction it blows, or stalwart prophets who, as Malachi spoke about, have been tested and found to be pure?

Today's scripture centers around John's question about who Jesus is, and Jesus' statements about who John is, but we also need to consider — just who is Malachi? His name means both "messenger" and "angel." That messenger, like John, came to prepare the way before the day of the Lord. It is a road that leads to a more satisfying relationship with God. It is one that will end well, because as it says in Malachi 3:4, once we get there, "... the offering of Judah and Jerusalem will be pleasing to the LORD as in the days of old and as in former years." Our good relationship with God will be restored.

The way involves a refiner's fire, purification, and testing, but when we have gone through the testing, which Jesus has shown we can endure, then we will be at peace with ourselves, and with God.

Prophets like John followed the example of their predecessors like Isaiah and Jeremiah, who wrote as the nation fell apart, as destruction loomed, as kings remained faithless to their faith and the people followed. Yet even as the prophets prophesized doom, they also foretold return. The vulnerable, the weak, the struggling will be strengthened. This journey is for them, Isaiah said. And how will they know the way?

There was a commercial many years ago about a product that was "so easy, even a caveman could do it." The caveman, far more sophisticated than he was given credit for, was insulted. Isaiah said "...no traveler, not even fools, shall go astray" (Isaiah

35:8). We are insulted if the term is applied to us. But it is used here to suggest that the road back from exile will be so easy even we can't get lost.

In our age of GPS and smart phones, we act as though it's nearly impossible for us to get lost, but still, we do. This verse suggests that with God's goodwill those of us marching to Zion will get there, no matter how we insist we're not going to ask for directions.

Is there a road back to normalcy?

Despite all appearances, Isaiah and Jesus were telling us the story is not over. There is a highway of return, which meant that the people had not hit the point of no return. This was God's doing, not our own, hence the term "the ransomed of the Lord."

Who will lead the ransomed? Okay, the answer is always Jesus. But the word in the Hebrew used in this passage is *go'el*, which sounds like something out of a Superman comic. And maybe it is. The Go'el, the redeemer, is the guy in the family you go to, to get things done. It's the uncle you go to for bail. It's the one who knows a guy who knows a guy at city hall. He's the fixer, not because he's dishonest, but because someone has to look out for the family. It might be the grandma or the aunt people rely on. It might be the youngest brother.

It's you. It's me.

Remember the Dr. Seuss story, *How the Grinch Stole Christmas*? Remember the ending? He didn't stop Christmas from coming, it came. Somehow or other it came just the same. What happened? Okay, I wasn't actually there, but I figure somebody in Whoville, once the shock wore off, said, "Okay, everyone, out in the quad. Why? We're singing Christmas songs. Why? Do you see any presents? Do you see any dinner? Anyone got a pressing engagement? Might as well sing, right?"

And it worked.

Think of the dad in *A Christmas Story*, after the neighbor's dogs eat the turkey and drag the carcass out onto the lawn, he said, "All right, everybody get dressed, we're going out," and they ended up eating Chinese food and having the best Christmas ever.

It's like my friend who's undergoing chemo right now, but during the winter of 1978 when all of us at Bethany Seminary were snowed in and couldn't get out, strapped on his cross country skis and came back with milk for all the kids. (PUT YOUR OWN EXAMPLE HERE)

You can bellyache about the pastor's sermons, you can complain about the government, or you can be the change someone needs in their life, the lifeline to someone isolated and alone, the bag of groceries on the doorstep, or the card in the mail with a verse of scripture.

The ransomed of the Lord will return because of me and you, and what we do. We have been living through a time of hatred and demonizing, where good people have decided that other good people are depraved. In response we can no longer be reeds shaking in the wind, but prophets standing tall. We know the way back to a *Charlie Brown Christmas*, to the shepherds, and to the infant king. Hark the herald angels sing! Be a super hero. Be a Go'El. Be a redeemer!

Amen.

Fourth Sunday of Advent
Matthew 1:18-25

Bare Stage

One of the best parts of Christmas is getting out the nativity set. There's often a family history behind the one in your home. Perhaps it belonged to your grandparents, or was given to you by a beloved aunt. Maybe there's a chip on Mary's arm or the leg of the baby Jesus, which tells a story about how you played with it as a child. Maybe there's a missing Magi, who has been replaced by a super hero action figure, by the kid who accidentally broke it, in the hopes you won't notice.

If our nativity sets were based on the birth story in Matthew's gospel instead of Luke's, it would be pretty empty. There would be no shepherds and no sheep. The birth wouldn't take place in a stable so there'd be no manger and no cows. The angels didn't appear to the shepherds, so no heavenly choir! Sure, Matthew told us about the Magi who came with camels after following the star — but they didn't appear for a couple of years. So out go the star, the wise men, and the camels.

As for Mary and the baby Jesus, they were offstage. We don't see them. Bye, bye!

So what are we left with?

A bare stage. And a man sleeping!

When we pay good money to see a play, a lot of us want to see bells and whistles — large set pieces, bells and whistles, loud noises, and lots of lighting effects. But as anyone involved in theater can tell you, a bare stage can sometimes be the most effective because there's nothing to distract you from the story. The power of the bare stage forces us to look at the actors and what they do, how they react to circumstances.

And our story is all about Jesus!

Except, as we said, there's no Jesus. The greatest miracle debuts out of sight — in Mary's pregnancy through the Holy Spirit.

Like I said, we would see a bare stage featuring Joseph, sleeping on a bed in whatever house he lived in.

Then. Action! An angel appeared.

Only it was in a dream, not filling the heavens with light, joy, and singing like in Luke, but talking. We don't see the angel. Only Joseph saw the angel.

All we have is Joseph, and whatever bed he slept on in whatever house he lived in. The voice of an angel, a disembodied voice, and Joseph stirred in the dream — and frowns. He heard the words.

What would happen next?

Ah, dreams. They are so vivid, so powerful, so real. Some dreams stick with us for life. Some dreams haunt us. Others fade away, so what we are left with are like a few dry leaves that are the remnant of an ancient autumn. The wind blows the leaves away and it's all gone.

Actually, Joseph had a series of dreams. He had the dream described in today's scripture, and a dream telling him to hightail it with his family to Egypt, and another dream instructing him it was time to return to his homeland.

What is the significance of Joseph's dreams? Certainly in the Bible, dreams can have meaning. Jacob was fleeing from his brother Esau to escape physical harm or even death, and while he slept in fear beneath a tree with a pillow for a stone, he dreamed about a ladder that stretched to the heavens with angels ascending and descending, and he called the place Bethel, house of God, because, as he said, surely the Lord is in this place and I did not know it.

Joseph was able to interpret other people's dreams. He understood the dreams of his fellow prisoners, the baker and the cupbearer, as well as Pharaoh's dreams about seven years of plenty and seven years of famine. His dreams brought him fame and fortune.

There was Daniel, whose dreams revealed that God is in charge of history, that dictators come and go, and empire has to bow before apocalypse.

One thing that's clear is that dreams require interpretation. We can evaluate them on our own, but Daniel prayed together with his friends Shadrach, Meshach, and Abednego. Creating a community of prayer when evaluating whatever might be God's leading, is a healthy practice.

I wonder if Joseph, alarmed that his fiancé was pregnant with a child not his own, talked over this dream with a friend, his parents, or his rabbi? I wonder if Joseph prayed about this dream alone, or called upon his friends to help answer questions like: Should I act on this? Should I file it away until I get some sign? What if this is the sign?

The thing is, even before the dream Joseph was already leaning toward righteousness. By the standards of his society, Mary's pregnancy brought shame to his family, since an engagement was as binding as a marriage. As it says in Deuteronomy 22:20-21, 23-24:

If, however, this charge is true, that evidence of the young woman's virginity was not found, then they shall bring the young woman out to the entrance of her father's house and the men of her town shall stone her to death, because she committed a disgraceful act in Israel by prostituting herself in her father's house. So you shall purge the evil from your midst. ... If there is a young woman, a virgin already engaged to be married, and a man meets her in the town and lies with her, you shall bring both of them to the gate of that town and stone them to death, the young woman because she did not cry for help in the town and the man because he violated his neighbor's wife. So you shall purge the evil from your midst.

We should still give Joseph credit. Even though he evidently didn't believe Mary's story at first, that she was a virgin even though she was obviously pregnant, and he knew very well that barring an unprecedented miracle there is only one way she could become pregnant, he nevertheless refused to obey the letter of the law and have Mary killed. He chose to divorce Mary quietly, doing less than the law demanded. He chose grace. In so doing, he opened the door to a miracle. All this was done before an angel spoke to him in a dream about the birth of a Savior. Joseph made a righteous, if counterintuitive, choice.

In the novel *Foundation* by Isaac Asimov, Salvor Hardin, mayor of Terminus, had a saying: "Never let your morals prevent you from doing what is right." There are times we are fully justified by the law of scripture and human laws to do our worst, but Jesus came to teach us about grace, opening the door for the Spirit of God to dwell fully in us and among us. Graciousness and unexpected kindness may be the best gift we can give each other this holiday season.

Jesus came to teach us about grace, about opening the door for God's Spirit to dwell fully in us and among us. That's the best gift we can give each other this holiday season. Give Joseph credit. Take a little credit for yourself. Give everyone some slack!

Now let's listen to what the angel said in the dream: "Joseph, son of David, do not be afraid to take Mary as your wife, for the child conceived in her is from the Holy Spirit. She will bear a son, and you are to name him Jesus, for he will save his people from their sins" (Matthew 1:20-21).

Notice the angel didn't actually do anything. The angel only told Joseph he should not be afraid to take Mary into his home as his wife, that she conceived by the Holy Spirit, and would bear a son who would save the people from their sins. Now that I think of it, the angel *did* give Joseph one task — to name the child Jesus, which means, "He rescues," or "He saves."

When all was said and done, it was still up to Joseph to act, to take Mary into his home and to be open to the possibility of a miracle. In order for Joseph to act in this manner, he would have to step away from fear.

Let me say that again. The dream from the angel inspired him to ignore the verses that were being quoted to him by friends and relatives, and people who love their clobber verses, and instead to listen to God, to God's great wonders, and in obeying God make it possible for God to enter into history and save the people.

In response, Joseph took action, and that action was to do the right thing. He would adopt Jesus as his own. He would bring joy to the world!

A bare stage brings a drama to life in *our* lives as well. We see ourselves more clearly when there are fewer distractions. We hear God more clearly as well. And the question for us, having seen this drama, is how do we know God is speaking to us, whether in our dreams, or through a sign or wonder, through scripture, or through a leading of the Holy Spirit?

Like Joseph, we need to evaluate the revelations we receive. One important step is to create a community of prayer with our friends and relatives, to talk to people, to hear what they saw, and to evaluate scriptures together. That is the core of what it means to be the church. We are called to read scripture together, talk about it, argue about it, pray together and pray about it, because we are not in this alone. We think we are. We act like we are. But we're all part of something bigger.

Because this is not just about Joseph and Mary and a little village in Galilee. It's bigger than all of us. Like Isaiah says, unto *us*, all of us, a child is born. The good news is that nothing can stop this holy day from coming. Maybe it wouldn't hurt to get rid of some of the clutter on our own stage, as we prepare for our own little drama!

We are not in this alone. That's what the name of Jesus means. Whether you call Jesus Emmanuel, which means: God with us, or Yeshua — the Lord saves, the Lord rescues — God is with us. God is with us in something as ordinary and messy as childbirth. God is with us in something that is the unique action of the Holy Spirit.

And we have something else to help us in addition to God's Holy Spirit and God's people. We have God's word.

Two thousand years ago, ancient Christians would write prayers and scriptures on a strip of papyrus (the ancient equivalent of paper) and wear them around their wrist or neck. This was called an "amulet." People drew strength from these prayers and scriptures. These might be often worn for specific ailments, such as headaches, or for protection against diseases such as the flu. Church authorities spoke out against the practice but there has always been a conflict between what church leaders say and what ordinary believers do.

Obviously, people in ancient times didn't have knowledge of germ theory or access to modern medical procedures. Still, while wearing a Bible verse might not actually prevent disease or cure headaches, it was kind of like chicken soup — couldn't hurt!

One amulet published recently included the words from Matthew 1:20: "Joseph, son of David, do not be afraid...", the very words spoken by the angel in a dream to reassure Joseph that his fiancé Mary's pregnancy was part of God's plan for salvation. Christians believed words spoken through an angel in a dream had great power, and who wouldn't want to share the emotional, spiritual, and/or physical healing that comes with the divine word?

There are times when fear holds us back from witnessing to the truth about Jesus, and against the lies of racism, nationalism, and materialism that pervade our society. We are still called to do the right thing, regardless of the clobber verses other people are quoting.

Christmas is about the intersection of the ordinary and the miraculous. This is where we live. This is us. We don't always have angels singing on high, signs and wonders, special effects, lighting, sound, and wonder. Sometimes it's a dream, a nudge, or a feeling. Sometimes it is on a bare stage or through a Zoom call!

But whether we listen or not, God's *will* shall be done, with us, or without us.

Just so you know, it's okay to get that nativity set with the shepherds and wise men, as well as the cows, camels, stars, manger, and Mary all mixed together. You don't have to put Joseph on a bed with an angel hovering over him, giving him a dream, in order to celebrate Christmas in your home.

Here's what it comes down to:

The world tells us -- the gospel is unbelievable.

Joseph believes.

The world tells us to fear.

The angel said, "Fear not."

The world tells us we're on our own.

The child is named Emmanuel, God with us.

Choose this day what you will believe, and if believing, how you will act.

The angel is speaking to us today —

It's up to us to respond!

It's about hearing God and acting on it. Joy to the world. The Lord is come! Jesus, God saves, Emmanuel, God is with us! Here is the infant king. O come, let us adore him.

Amen.

What's In A Word?

Do you know what I mean when I use the term "bathrobe biblical"? I'm talking about the way we dress the kids for the Christmas pageant at church — old bathrobes become robes for Joseph, Grandpa's cane becomes a shepherd's crook, and a cigar box gets decorated with gold-painted macaroni so the kings have a treasure to bring.

If you remember cigar boxes, you're dating yourself. The traces of that deep, pungent smell were every bit as mysterious as frankincense and myrrh.

These images created in our pageants are so powerful. And whether it is read by a narrator, or acted out in one of those Las Posadas Pageants that are part of Christmas for so many of us, one of the most important plot twists is there was no room in the inn, so Jesus was born in a barn.

That Jesus was born in a barn, or at least something like a stable is a staple of our Christmas celebrations. Every nativity set is set in a barn with animals. Oh, sometimes people will call it a cave, but that's just another word for a stony barn.

That image of "no room at the inn!" is so ingrained in us, perhaps because we can all relate to an experience in which someone took us in or helped us out, or when we went the extra mile for someone truly in need. This biblical image sometimes powerfully pushes us to reluctant but effective action.

And of course, on the negative side, perhaps we remember when someone who could have helped refused, and left us in the cold. Or could there be a guilty memory for us, sometime, when we didn't answer the phone because we were afraid it was a call for help? Hmmm…

Too bad it's nowhere near what actually happened….

If you're a *Monty Python* fan, you're familiar with the phrase, "Nobody expects the Spanish Inquisition!" That's one of *Monty Python's* most famous lines. A lot of people have their favorite skit from that groundbreaking British sketch comedy series. Some favor the dead parrot sketch. Others prefer the one about the cheese shop. The Spanish Inquisition sketch features normal folks getting questioned by a relative, only to have a mustachioed clergyman bursting on the scene shouting the tagline, "Nobody expects the Spanish Inquisition!"

In the sketch the inquisitors subject their victims to torture devices like "the comfy chair" or the "soft pillow." If people didn't expect a Spanish Inquisition they certainly didn't expect this sort of treatment either.

But the Spanish Inquisition was no joke. It had free license to torture and maim anyone it chose in order to determine if they were guilty of a crime heinous enough to burn people alive!

In 1584, a professor named Francisco Sánchez de las Brozas, better known as "El Borcense," was turned in to the Spanish Inquisition by his students. They didn't do it simply to get out of class. They turned him in on a charge of heresy.

El Borcense was a professor of philology. That meant he taught the history and meaning of words. What words could he teach about that were so heretical that he fell into the hands of the notorious Spanish Inquisition?

Simply this: he was arrested by the Spanish Inquisition because he said the depictions of the Nativity in church paintings were all wrong. He insisted the language of Luke 2:7 — "And she gave birth to her firstborn son and wrapped him in bands of cloth, and laid him in a manger, because there was no place for them in the inn" — was not correctly translated.

Jesus was *not* born in a stable because some innkeeper had a heart of stone. Nor were his folks turned away by an innkeeper because there was no room. Mary gave birth in a private home, probably belonging to Joseph's relatives.

The Greek word *kataluma,* often translated as "inn," refers to a "guest room" built on the roof of a typical Judean home that could be used by company, by adult sons and their families as the larger family got bigger, or for guests who dropped in. Elsewhere in the gospel of Luke it is translated as "upper room" as in the guest room where the Last Supper is served. No one ever suggested the Last Supper was served in an "inn."

What was happening, El Borcense said, was that Joseph and Mary would have been given the upstairs room when they arrived at his family home in Bethlehem for the census, when, as Luke tells us, "All went to their own towns to be registered" (Luke 2:3).

However, that room was totally inadequate when Mary went into labor. The midwives would have been called by the family. She would have been helped downstairs, or perhaps down a ladder. They would have helped her walk around, breathe, sit just right, as they guided her through the birth process.

The thing is, even though it got him arrested, he was right.

Most experts have known it. They understood the archaeology of the houses in first-century Bethlehem. They understood the words. Yet for the most part, most translations stuck with the idea that there were inns, innkeepers, and a stable involved the way we think of them in this story!

There are exceptions. The 1385 Wycliffe Bible got it right when it used the phrase: "there was no place to him in no chamber."

But William Tyndale's groundbreaking 1526 translation set the standard when he chose these words: "ther was no roume for them within in the ynne."

Most translations, including the King James Version, followed Tyndale's example. In our time, the very influential New Revised Standard and New International Versions both use the word "inn."

But Today's New International Version in 2005 says "…there was no guest room available for them." The 2010 Common English Bible says "…there was no place for them in the guest room."

How should it be translated? Something like this: "She gave birth to her firstborn child, a son, wrapped him snugly, and laid him in a manger because they had no space in their place to stay."

Where was Jesus born?

Like I've been saying, at home!

This fits nicely with what is known about the architecture of the typical Palestinian home of the period. There was usually a single large room. The sleeping, cooking, and family craft work took place there. Animals shared the living space, dwelling on a portion of the floor slightly lower than the people. They were, after all, an essential part of the family economy.

In a typical village in Judea or Galilee, or anywhere else in the ancient world, houses were packed close together. Families, therefore, did not add a new room on the ground floor. There was no room. Instead they expanded upward. They built a *kataluma* on the roof, accessible through either an outdoor staircase or an indoor ladder. When Joseph brought his pregnant fiancée home to Bethlehem, his family built an upper room for the newlyweds. But when Mary went into labor she was moved downstairs because there wasn't enough room in the *kataluma* upstairs. The feeding trough of the animals was close at hand since they lived there too. It served as a bed for the newborn Jesus.

Remember that Mary, the mother of Mark, for instance, built an upper room on her home in Jerusalem that was used by Jesus and the apostles for the Last Supper. It was where the apostles and the women waited while Jesus was dead and buried, and where Jesus appeared to them after his resurrection. It's where the Holy Spirit descended at Pentecost, and where Peter went after an angel helped him escape from prison. None of that happened in an inn. All of it happened in an upper room.

Consider this — Joseph was from Bethlehem. He had relatives in Bethlehem. Everyone lived together. Everyone went to their home town for the census. This was Joseph's home town. It might have even been his house. Perhaps he was planning to settle there with Mary. Why *wouldn't* he plan on living there after his marriage to a Galilean girl?

They didn't return, however, to Nazareth after the birth of Jesus. Later, Herod commanded that all boys two years and younger be killed, many think that's how old Jesus was when the Magi arrived. This has caused some to think it was likely enough Joseph and Mary intended to live in Bethlehem permanently.

The more likely scenario is that Joseph was a Bethlehem boy engaged to a Nazareth girl in an arranged marriage. His family evidently built a small room on the roof for the newlyweds, but when it was time for Jesus to be born the room was too small for childbirth so they moved downstairs, and used the family manger for his bed. Luke had it right. We had it translated wrong.

Before I go any further, don't go out and bust up your nativity set. Nor do we need to construct new ones. This is the way we tell the story, and there are many good lessons to be learned from being read this way, in case strangers knock on our door, as Joseph and Mary have been depicted as doing in all the stories about the birth of Jesus.

Now you may ask, does it matter?

Short answer — Yes.

Because for centuries we've criticized the self-centered inn keepers who couldn't find room for Mary and Joseph when they found themselves far from home in a confusing town during a busy time.

But really, the story is about a family planning to take care of its own, and reverting to Plan B when it was necessary.

We should do be ready to do the same. Instead of blaming someone else because there isn't room for visitors, it's up to us to make room for grandma when she can't live alone anymore, or perhaps as grandparents it's up to us to take care of our children's children on occasion.

That's part of the joy of Luke's story. Everyone was exactly where they ought to have been, and everybody was ready to adjust their lives — and their sleeping arrangements — once things changed.

The same is expected of us! We are all meant to be in our places, for the drama that is unfolding in our families. We can't always have dinner at the normal time. We may be called to pick up children from school when they're sick. We may become the grandparents who are raising their children.

That's just our immediate family. We may be called to stand up for children in our society, and beyond our comfort zone.

Not everyone's home is flexible enough to accommodate a modern day upper room, which doesn't need to be upstairs. But there's there the family of God comes in. Are our church structures ready to provide hospitality outside of these four walls? Are we ready to help in the case of an emergency in our community, such as a tornado, flooding, or fire? Can we move things around so that people can move into our spaces, so that a community choir or a food bank finds a place here? Or are there too many sacred cows?

As the family of Christ we are meant to take care of each other.

By the way, if you're worried about El Borcense, the first time he was arrested his powerful patron helped get him released. Later, after that patron died, he was arrested once more by the Inquisition for criticizing all the paintings of the birth of Jesus in the churches, and was put under house arrest until his death. But he seems to have escaped some of the brutal excesses of the Spanish Inquisition.

The Christmas story is a story of inconvenience. It involved pain, blood, and joy, as is the case with every childbirth. It stretched the potential of a living space and made it the more holy than anyone at the time could possibly have imagined. And it happened in an ordinary neighborhood. If your house is stretched to its limit with family and friends, if people are sleeping wall to wall in your apartment, and if you're the reason someone's sleeping on the couch because you're in the guestroom, take heart! You're following in some very impressive footsteps and this may be the most Christmasy Christmas you've ever celebrated.

Amen!

(Want to know more? Read "The Accommodations of Joseph and Mary in Bethlehem: καταλύμα in Luke 2.7," by Stephen

The Real World

Hello Pastor. For Nativity of the Lord — Proper 2, I have gath-
ered three sermonettes, if your Christmas service centers around a large
pageant, a cantata, or an elaborate set of readings with candles, some-
thing that leaves you only a few minutes for a brief message, you will
find that brief message in these pages.

For some, the story of Christmas is a fantasy set in an idealized world where pregnant women get to ride donkeys while
prophets look into a deep future divorced from the day's reali-
ties. It's a world defined by the lyrics of Christmas carols and the
illustrations on Christmas cards. But the real world is far more
interesting and exciting, and the birth of Jesus took place in a real
world, where desperate situations demanded even more than in
peaceful times that we act righteously according to God's word,
with the expectation that God's good will shall be accomplished
in our own life's struggles.

In a world where a distant imperial power could move people around like pieces on a chess board, where shepherds didn't
own their own sheep and were reviled because of their economic
misfortune, this story took place. It was a world where a young
pregnant woman had to walk three days to arrive at her husband's home town in order to be registered, then gave birth to a
child who was everything Isaiah foresaw. When God sent angels
to announce this birth they were sent not to emperors, kings, or
religious authorities, but to those poor, ornery shepherds — that
was what happened in the real world!

This holiday season, let's pretend there's more than one present under the Christmas sermon tree. I hope these vignettes will
help put things in perspective as we keep one foot in the real
world and the other firmly planted in God's holy history.

Roman Holiday

In those days a decree went out from Emperor Augustus that all the world should be registered.... All went to their own towns to be registered (Luke 2:1, 3).

Nobody saved a copy of the decree from Caesar Augustus, but here's an interesting document written in Egypt in 104 AD, calling on everyone to return to their home districts to be counted for the census.

Gaius Vibius Maximus, the Roman Governor over Egypt is saying:

Since the house-to-house census has started it is proclaimed that anyone currently living outside their home district be required to come back to their home so the census can be completed, so the farmers can get back to cultivating their allotted plots.

However, I know that some country people are needed in the city, so if you have a satisfactory excuse for staying here during the census you should....(gap in the papyrus).

Those who must stay in the city should get signed permits from Festus, the Roman Calvary Commander, according to the manner prescribed in this edict by the 30th of this month.

As you can see, there is a requirement for people to travel to their home districts to be registered for the census, but some people had permission to stay put.

This is the kind of thing we expect from the Roman Empire, but how about our own holidays in the land of the free and the home of the brave? How many young families feel free to stay home for Christmas and start traditions of their own? Are there occasions a matriarch and/or patriarch hold family members emotional hostage with their own census summons? No matter how complicated the circumstances or how far away people live, they're told their absence will ruin the holidays. Kids cry because they don't want to leave their new toys, but cars are packed and go over the river and through the woods to grandmother's house.

What are the rules in your family for Christmas? Who makes them? Are you the rule maker? What exceptions do you allow?

The first Christmas might have gone a lot easier if Joseph and Mary had been able to celebrate the birth of their first child in Nazareth. And things might have gone easier if the Magi had been able to follow the star to Galilee instead of traveling to Jerusalem to unintentionally awaken the savage suspicions of a King Herod.

Let us travel to visit each other because we sincerely wish to, not because we have to. Let's be family in many different ways.

(This is my translation of Papyrus British Museum, London, no. 904.)

Quirinius versus Christ

In those days a decree went out from Emperor Augustus that all the world should be registered. This was the first registration and was taken while Quirinius was governor of Syria. (Luke 2:1-2)

The ancient Roman historian Tacitus interrupted his account of the political and military intrigues of the year 20 AD to dish about a salacious divorce trial that transfixed all of Rome. Aemilia Lepeda, a member of one of the great noble houses, was sued for divorce by her husband Publius Sulpicius Quirinius. He was a high-ranking official who had distinguished himself as a procurator, governor, protector, and for his military exploits, but though he had three names, befitting one of high rank, he was really a commoner.

And yes — this is the same Quirinius mentioned in Luke 2:2 at the opening of the famous Nativity story!

He was "a childless old millionaire" according to Tacitus. There were accusations of adultery, and charges he hired astrologers to get dirt on the imperial family. Aemilia's brother took up her defense, and at first gained his sister's great sympathy through the way he portrayed her, while heaping scorn on her accuser.

At one point, the trial was interrupted by public games. Aemilia used the occasion to weep and wail, protesting her innocence in public, causing the crowd, in the words of the historian, to insult Quirinius as "a dirty, low-class, childless, old man...." while lamenting that Aemilia should have been married to Lucius Caesar and become the daughter-in-law of Augustus Caesar instead of getting stuck with Quirinius!

Alas, further investigation revealed that Aemilia had tried to poison her husband. Public opinion turned on a dime, as did the scales of justice, and although she was not stripped of her possessions, she did lose out in both the courts of law and public opinion.

Not much later Quirinius died, having lived a full life of 72 years. Tiberius Caesar requested that the Senate accord him all the honors of a state funeral. As Tacitus pointed out, this man had no connections with any of the ancient and noble families, and "...even though he had the name of that prestigious clan, having come from bourgeois stock in Lanuvium, he was a good general, and had a distinguished record of service under Augustine. That won him the consulship and an honorary triumph in capturing the fortresses of the Homonadenses in Cilicia." The latter victory settled a decades-long score with the people of that region, who had driven out the Romans in a rare, humiliating defeat. And though there were those who still thought of him as "an avaricious old man who wielded more power than he should, and who still favored his ex-wife, his service in the Syria province and Judea was not forgotten."

One of the events of his reign which is alluded to in the Bible was chronicled by the Jewish historian Josephus who recalled that when Quirinius was governor of the Syrian province a census was held, military zealots had rebelled, and their rebellion was quelled by this same Quirinius. This event was recalled by the famed teacher of the law, Gamaliel, under whom Paul learned Torah. In Acts 5:37, while recounting failed messiahs, Gamaliel said, "...Judas the Galilean rose up at the time of the census and got people to follow him; he also perished, and all who followed him were scattered."

This has caused biblical historians some problems. Quirinius was governor of Syria, which included Judea and therefore Bethlehem, from 6 to 12 AD. However, we're told by Matthew that Jesus was born during the reign of Herod the Great, who is thought to have died in 4 BC. That's a big chronological gap.

Some have wondered if Quirinius had served twice as governor. Others think Luke was mistaken about Quirinius.

In her 2019 book *Papyri and the Social World of the New Testament* Sabine R. Heuber made an interesting suggestion. After giving several examples of actual census forms preserved in Egypt of the Roman census, she pointed out that only early Christian writers from the second century mentioned the census held at the time of the birth of Jesus. Both had Roman connections and both could have checked official records. Justin Martyr, writing to a Roman skeptic, pointed out the census took place under the administration of the procurator (Latin, *duumvir*) Quirinius. Tertullian said that the census took place under the governor Saturnius, who reigned over the Syrian Province from 8 to 6 BC, just about the right time.

That means that Saturnius may have been the governor while Quirinus was the Levie Procurator, which meant the latter had financial responsibility during those years. The words in Luke bear this out. *Hegemon,* the Greek word translated now as governor, meant procurator. Elsewhere in the New Testament the real Greek word for governor is strategus.

No problem after all!

The odds are good that regardless of your age, you've heard Luke's Christmas story read aloud many times. You've heard the name Quirinius many times, and probably neither knew a thing about him, nor cared that you didn't, either. To be honest, it's legitimate to ask the question, what does it matter anyway?

It matters that it doesn't matter. When Luke wrote the gospel he mentioned Quirinius because everyone knew about him because of the divorce scandal. His service as governor or procurator was a great landmark to place Jesus in the larger scheme of things. But as it turned out, Jesus is now a much better landmark to date people like Augustus Caesar and Governor Quirinius.

That should make us all wonder, what public figures who command constant attention, whose scandals dominate headlines, and whose every action and every word is relayed breathlessly around our world will truly matter a hundred years, a decade, a year, or even a month from now? Whereas the birth of Jesus is celebrated the world over, even among non-believers. And will, barring his return, still be important 2,000 years from now.

(Quotations from Tacitus come from "The Annals of Tacitus: A Modern New Translation by Donald R. Dudley," New American Library, 1966, with reference to "Tacitus: The Annals," translated by Alfred John Church and William Jackson Brodgribb, The University of Chicago Great Books, 1952. "Papyri and the Social World of the New Testament," by Sabine R. Huebner was published by Cambridge University Press in 2019.)

"That's what Christmas is all about, Charlie Brown."

And the angel said unto them, Fear not: for, behold, I bring you good tidings of great joy, which shall be to all people. For unto you is born this day in the city of David a Savior, which is Christ the Lord. And this shall be a sign unto you; Ye shall find the babe wrapped in swaddling clothes, lying in a manger (Luke 2:10-12, KJV).

It's hard to imagine now but the network executives who commissioned the half-century old classic *"A Charlie Brown Christmas"* believed they had a turkey on their hands. Their marketers told them the final product was awful. They insisted the story-line was thin, the music was forgettable, and the scene where Linus recites the Christmas story from Luke ought to be cut. In the end they let the cartoon special alone because they figured they'd show it once and everyone would forget about it.

How wrong they were. The show is a classic. Vince Guaraldi's music is part of everyone's personal soundtrack. The scene where Linus recites from Luke's gospel demonstrates just how powerful this story is even after nearly two thousand years.

It was no less powerful when Luke first wrote down his account. He began by telling us who was emperor in Rome and who was the governor of the Syria province, and then he tossed them out of the tale. They may be at the center of imperial power, but they were not important to God's story! A pregnant Palestinian teenager whose story would be hard to swallow in any age, along with her fiancé, traveled three days to his home village near Jerusalem near Jerusalem, thereby fulfilling the prophecy about where the Messiah would be born. There was no room at the inn, but likely there was room at the home of Bethlehem residents who were originally from Nazareth and who probably housed the young couple along with others from their home town. Like many homes of the era, it was a one room structure in which the valuable animals slept on the lower part of the floor while up just a few inches on the other side the people slept. The woman went into birth at the worst possible time, but there's no stopping a baby. The birth announcement was given by angels not to political or religious authorities, but unto shepherds, who, thanks to a recent debt crisis, has probably gone bankrupt and now watched other people's sheep. Once their profession was honored and kings were compared to shepherds but shepherds were pretty much the least trusted people, and it was to such as these that the angels appeared!

You can see how this story could be filmed as a comedy or a tragedy. What the story truly can be described as is a triumph! It was God's triumph, but also the triumph of humans and their choices — Mary who said *yes*, Joseph who said *no* to shaming Mary, shepherds who obeyed the angels and proclaimed the good news of the gospel for the first time, and so on.

In the real world we have to make choices. But in the real world there is also the grace of God. All will be well.

Merry Christmas — and may God bless us, everyone!

Amen.

The Prequel

When a large-screen super-colossal action-picture is every bit the success its makers hoped, you know there's going to be another movie. The next movie can jump ahead, continuing the story, showing us what comes next. That's a sequel.

Or it can jump backward, to the past, and let us see what happened before the movie we just saw. That's called a prequel. I'm not sure if prequel is really a word, but I've heard it so often I'm pretty sure it almost certainly has to be one by now.

Why a prequel, when most of us want to know what happens next to our hero? I guess to let us know what made our hero who they are today. Maybe it is to let us know where our hero comes from and why she or he responds the way they do. Perhaps it is to get insight on what's going to happen next by knowing what happened at first.

John's gospel is the Christmas prequel. It doesn't cover the same territory that Matthew and Luke charted. We don't huddle in the cold with the shepherds when suddenly the sky turns all angels, or follow the star like the Magi. Nor do we go to the next chapter, where we might see the toddler Jesus take his first steps, say his first word, or perform his first miracle.

No, we go back, back, back, to Genesis 1 — before creation.

Just to remind you, creation begins with light. "In the beginning." The Hebrew word that starts off Genesis 1:1 with a big bang (so to speak) is *bereshet,* a word referring to good order and good foundations when it comes to building. Genesis pictures an orderly creation. Ours is not a cosmos teetering on the edge of chaotic dissolution at any moment. Though it is far from a safe universe (cf. black holes, meteor airbursts, and yet another boy band), it is a secure universe.

Likewise, John opened his gospel with the Greek word *arche*, which means beginning or foundation, upon which everything depends. Just as Genesis was about how creation was not slip-shod or unwieldy but orderly as well as creative, so too John told us the foundation of this orderly cosmos, the world, is wise, measured, logical, and thoughtful. Darkness was dispelled by light. All was well.

Darkness and light. It's a consistent theme in scripture. Terrifying darkness, metaphorically speaking, but just hold on and wait a spell. God's light will restore and renew the hopes and fortunes of the people. *For darkness shall cover the earth, and thick darkness the peoples; but the Lord will arise upon you, God's glory will appear over you* (Isaiah 60:2).

Sometimes it takes longer than others for restoration to occur. Especially when something happens of biblical proportions. Darkness strikes, and it might take six or seven centuries for life and hope to be restored, for crops to grow and people to return.

Six or seven hundred years?

That's right. Evidently 3,700 years ago, around 1700 BC, a large object, perhaps an asteroid or a meteor, struck the earth's atmosphere and exploded around half a mile above present-day Jordan, instantly destroying all the cities and towns over a two-hundred square mile stretch. Temperatures rose momentarily to 18,000 degrees. 40,000 to 60,000 people died instantly. Pottery turned to glass. Buildings were torn off their moorings. This once rich agricultural region was poisoned by the salty brackish waters of the north end of the Dead Sea, which were strewn all over the area.

Those outside the death zone were no doubt awestruck and terrified by the event. Later those few who worked up the courage to investigate would have seen a dead landscape where nothing would grow for half a millennium.

One of those who might have seen this blast could have been Abraham. He lived around 1700 BC and what he might have seen was the destruction of the cities of the plain, including towns like Sodom and Gomorrah.

Archaeologist Steven Collins of Trinity Southwest University in Albuquerque, New Mexico, and his colleague Philip Silvia insist the site of Tall el-Hamman in Jordan matched the cities of the plain as described in Genesis. The destruction matches what would have happened with an airburst caused by an astronomical event, not an earthquake or other natural cause. Pottery sherds turned to glass and high levels of platinum 600 % higher than normal are consistent with a cosmic airburst. The waters were displaced, poisoning the soil, would explain why it took centuries for people to return. The fact that a relatively small area of 200 square miles suggests that this airburst occurred only a half mile above the surface of the planet.

But cosmic catastrophe, as horrifying as may have been for those like Abraham to witness from a distance, and later to approach with dread and fear, was healed over time, as soils were renewed, life was restored, people returned, and new stories arise. This is part of what the prequel shows us — the fact that the word was present in the beginning means the story wasn't over. It was built on a firm foundation.

Contrast this horrifyingly bright light that certainly terrified the surrounding nations for hundreds of miles in all directions, with the light that called the nations to seek God's glory and wisdom, "the true light, which enlightens everyone, was coming into the world," as celebrated in this prequel to the birth of Jesus (John 1:9).

From the get go Jesus, *the Word*, was a part of this orderly creative process, essential to the nature of the cosmos. God spoke: "Let there be light!" and it was so. Before there were sun, moon, and stars, before the lights shone in the heaven, God spoke. John's gospel took us back to that moment and shined a light on the light, so to speak, so that we might see that in the very word that is spoken in *the* word. The word, which is the Greek word *logos,* is not only present in the beginning, but is active in the process of creation. The word is the way God works in creation. The Word *is* God. Nothing is made without the word.

God is a God of words. God spoke creation into being. God spoke the law on Mount Sinai. God's word was our guide to life.

The word is logical, deliberate, and responsible for this being a secure creation built on a firm foundation.

It soon becomes apparent that the Word *is* Jesus. Jesus *is* the light shining for all people. This light, John told us, shined in the darkness and the darkness was incapable of extinguishing it. Some won't recognize the light, but those who do get it are children of God. Typically, we think of light as blinding, and a bright light as part of something destructive, but this divine light becomes human and dwelt among us. We see God clearly. It is a light to which we all have access, and if we don't get it, it's our own fault for not seeing.

The first chapter of John assured us that this Word was there in the beginning, and that Jesus was and is how we see God.

The light shines for all! In this passage, the universal nature of this gift is reemphasized. The light of Christ, revealed in the infant Jesus, is proclaimed for all. We saw at Christmas that shepherds, on the margin of society, are the first to receive the good news of Jesus Christ. Augustus Kaiser was emperor but Jesus reigned.

This was bigger than we could imagine. God's plan of adoption and inclusion in the inheritance of Jesus Christ was for all. We are all going to be a part of this. This is mind-blowingly wonderful! The light of the world shines for all!

Moreover, that light shines in the darkness, and the darkness cannot overcome it. Remember the darkness that followed the great light of the cosmic event 1,700 years ago? Despite the catastrophic results that followed it was only a matter of time until the light returned, until healing slowly began, until human habitation became possible again.

Light is apparent for all to see, but whether we get it or not, the light shines in the darkness and the darkness cannot overcome it.

Nothing can make you open your eyes to see the light, if you choose to ignore it. Part of this prequel, part of this *before the birth — before the universe* story is the recognition that some people who ought to know better rejected Jesus. We're told "... the world did know him." Indeed, the ones described as "his own" "did not accept him." Jesus revealed himself as the way, the truth, and the life. And through Pilate, when Jesus had him bamboozled and confused during his trial, putting Pilate on the spot, the governor said, "What is truth?" in a way that suggests there's no way we can know truth.

The truth is right in front of us. This mighty passage concluded: "And *the Word* became flesh and dwelt among us, and we have seen his glory...."

So there *is* truth. There is a way. There is life. Truth is knowable, and if you want to be one of those the light cannot reach, then you may be caught up in the destruction that follows, as surely as happened when the great cosmic event 1,700 years ago unfolded.

Don't forget. John also said that, "to all who received him, who believed in his name, he gave power to become children of God...." Those are the stakes here.

Though calamitous events of biblical proportion happened in biblical times, there not limited to that time period. It's not unheard of for calamities like these to happen. It nearly happened again only recently on a far smaller scale on February 15, 2013, when an airburst caused by a meteor occurred over the city of Chelyabinks, Russia, damaging over 7,000 buildings and injuring 1,600 people.

A much more spectacular example occurred on June 30, 1908, over Tunguska, Siberia. That blast occurred around six miles above the earth. More than eighty million trees were blown over. Had this occurred over Europe instead of the isolated regions of Siberia, millions would have been killed.

One of the things that happened after a calamity is the arrival of relief, reconstruction, and the return of hope. The prophet Jeremiah lived through calamitous political times, that resulted in the destruction of Jerusalem, the temple, and the nation because of a failure to prepare, not for a natural catastrophe, but a crisis in faith. In Jeremiah 31:7-14, the prophet assured the nation, though they were on the brink of captivity that they would return, and the return would include those on the margins of society, the throwaways who might be neglected because of their vulnerability — the blind, the lame, the pregnant, and those giving birth.

It's worth noting in the midst of all the joyful dancing and music making in this passage, in the midst of all the celebration and homecoming, Jeremiah told us "With weeping they shall come, and with consolations I will lead them back…" (Jeremiah 31:9). To me, this is a reminder that though we preach a gospel of joy, people with PTSD, those with depression, and chronic pain, are still suffering, even as we celebrate all around them. They may wear a smile for our benefit but their pain is real and must be acknowledged. Jeremiah emphasized we should "…let them walk…in a straight path in which they shall not stumble…." (Jeremiah 31:9) bearing in mind their infirmities and making their paths easier, not harder.

Though the prophet Jeremiah had been warning of a national calamity that was on the way, in this passage there was the promise that God's love for us would ensure that regardless of our sins which had led to loss and alienation, all would be well. The nation will be returned, our losses will be restored, because God is compassionate. This is a message of hope and redemption.

This restoration is not just for the strong, the survivors, or the favored few. Among those the prophet described that the Lord would restore from the northland were the blind, lame, pregnant women, and those in actual labor. Now those were the ones who might have been excluded because their inclusion would slow the return. Valuable resources would have to be used for those individuals who could not care for themselves. We are not the people of God without everyone.

Our rock, our anchor, in calamity and calm, is the Word. That's the word usually translated as "dwelt" in John 1:14 and it comes from the Greek word *skene*, or "tent." (Tents were made from animal skins. See how we get the word "skin" from "*skene*"?) The word became flesh and "tented" among us. Unlike Moses, who was raised in Pharaoh's household, Jesus was born to a teenager in a Palestinian village on the edge of the Roman Empire. God roughed it, taking on human form.

Since "skene" can mean tent, it also reminds us of the tent that was the home of that most holy Ark of the Covenant, which traveled with the people through the desert. When they were starving, thirsting, complaining, God was with them. When King David wanted to build a mighty temple, God through the prophet Nathan reminded David that a tent had always been good enough.

"Skene" also looks like the word "scene," with good reason. The "skene" was also the theatrical backdrop made of animal skins in Greek drama. Jesus is part of a great drama, a tragedy and catastrophe which turns out to have a happy ending, what Tolkien called a "eucatastrophe," or good plot turn.

When we are enduring catastrophe, remember God has roughed it with us, tented in our midst, endured what we endure, and walks with us to this day. God is not a tourist, just passing through and taking selfies without really looking at all the people. God is not seated on a high throne, laughing at our follies and stirring the pot to see what happens when boredom strikes. God is one of us. The Word that is the foundation of order in our universe, the light which enlightens all nations, has walked through the worst the world has to offer and knows our sorrows, our pains, personally. That's what happens in the prequel to the Nativity. That's why we can trust the sequel, the cross, and *its* sequel, the resurrection, are our stories as well.

What is our guarantee that this will work and will be worth it? There's a phrase that's repeated throughout this chapter and heads this particular section — "Thus said the Lord!" We're all a part of God's plan. And if we're part of God's plan for restoration, we're all a part of God's church right now. The hymn of the Word in the first chapter of John assured us that this Word was there in the beginning, and though that Jesus was revealed for all the world, not all were ready to recognize him yet, but Jesus was and is how we see God. The light is shining in the darkness, and whether or not God's own recognize the light, others will.

The Word made flesh was not an accident. This was God's plan, coming to fruition over centuries, and happening in a rush in one place, at one moment in time, for everybody, everywhere. Mary, Joseph, shepherds, angels, and all of creation — I love it when a plan comes together! This was God's plan! Places! What's your place on stage? Are you ready for your part? Did you learn your part? Because it's all rushing fast to its fulfillment.

Amen.

(Want to know more? Enter *"Silvia and Collins, "The Civilization-Ending 3.7KYrBP Event: Archaeological Data, Sample Analyses, and Biblical Implications"* in a search engine to read the paper.)

Two Saviors

Every four years for seven and a half centuries, the heralds were sent forth from the sacred Mount Olympus to announce a sacred truce throughout the Greek-speaking world, so that athletes, dignitaries, and spectators could gather for the Olympic games. Thousands would answer the call. Wars were put on hold. People travelled safely over hundreds of miles to the sacred mountain. There they would witness the greatest athletes of the age engage in footraces, field events such as the long jump, the discus, and the javelin, as well various types of wrestling. The most brutal was called the Pankraton, an almost no-holds-barred battle (well, no eye gouging) that ended only when one combatant slapped the ground in surrender.

The victors won incredible prizes, including annuities for life. The games, after all, were anything but amateur. Champions were immortalized in poetry. Statues were raised. Their names were etched in rolls of honor. Nothing prevented these sacred games from taking place.

Until 12 BC.

The Roman civil wars that followed the assassination of Julius Caesar stretched resources so thin it looked as if the games would have to be canceled! A disaster loomed.

Ah, but then there arose the savior of the Olympics. He was acknowledged by other rulers throughout the Roman Empire as a great king. He had the favor of the Emperor in Rome. Statues attesting to his glory were raised among the nations. His gardens were considered innovative, transforming arid desert into lush and verdant landscape. He was widely admired among the rich and powerful for his great architectural achievements, not the least of which was finishing a temple whose construction had been stalled for centuries, making it one of the great wonders of the ancient world.

And he had the cash. Yes, Herod the Great, King of Judea, was fabulously wealthy. That wealth was built on the backs of his tormented subjects, who hated him with a fierceness that did not fade with his death.

Thanks to his generous financial gifts bankrolling the games, Herod the Great was hailed as the savior of the Olympics of 12 BC. He was awarded the unprecedented title of "President of the Games."

But Herod's greatness was recognized only by his fellow rulers. The people over whom he reigned, Galileans and Judeans alike, feared and hated him. Paranoid and besotted with suspicion, Herod was not above killing his own relatives in order to maintain power. Absolutely no one would supplant him, as far as he was concerned.

Today's gospel passage records one of the most horrifying acts in scripture — Herod's slaughter of innocent children because he feared one would grow up to be king is typical of his atrocities.

As Matthew told the story, the magi, arrived from the east, asking, "Where is the child who has been born king of the Jews? For we observed his star at its rising, and have come to pay him homage" (Matthew 2:2). These astrologers spent the nights stargazing, interpreting the signs they saw for the benefit of the powerful. Though we do not know exactly what it was they saw — there are many theories — what they saw in the eastern skies impelled them to travel a great distance to Judea and Jerusalem, its capital.

One of the most compelling stories (described in the book *The Christmas Star* written by astronomer John Mosley) revolved around an astonishing conjunction that occurred in August of 3 BC, and repeated in February and May of 2 BC: Jupiter, the king planet, and Venus, the queen planet, appeared to touch each other. This happened near Regulus, the king star, which is part of the constellation Leo, the Lion, and associated in the ancient world with the lion of Judah. The Magi could have easily interpreted this to mean a great king would be born in Judea. What more logical place could there have been for the Magi to seek that king but in the capital of Judea, Jerusalem?

Some dated the death of Herod in 4 BC, which would make this scenario impossible, but according to the historian Josephus, Herod the Great died in his madness between a total lunar eclipse and the Passover that followed. The only eclipse that fits the bill occurred on January 9 of 1 BC. Passover followed April of that year. Between May of 2 BC and April of 1 BC the Magi who responded would have had time to travel to Judea.

Herod's courtiers missed the celestial sign completely, but then, they were not star gazers. They had to think quickly when Herod asked them where this new Messiah was to be born. No doubt in fear of their paranoid and murderous king they answered his question about where this newborn king would be found, by turning to a verse from the prophet Micah to draw Herod's attention away from themselves and the holy city, to turn his wrath upon a small village a few miles away from Jerusalem.

Our nativity sets show the arrival of the magi, kneeling before the infant king in his manger, though this happened months after Jesus was born. We presume this because once Herod realized the Magi, having been warned in a dream not to return to Jerusalem but to go home a different way, were not going to bring him the mailing address of the newborn king, he ordered in his rage the slaughter of all male children two years old and younger.

Although later Christian writers would suggest this meant the slaughter of tens of thousands, or even hundreds of thousands of children, more recent writers, taking the population of Bethlehem into account and extrapolating the actual number of male children in a town of that size, suggested the number of children who were killed was probably closer to twenty. Still one would have been too many; it was an incalculable tragedy for each family and neighborhood.

Meanwhile "an angel of the Lord appeared to Joseph in a dream and said, 'Get up, take the child and his mother, and flee to Egypt . . .' " (Matthew 2:13). Most of us don't think of Jesus and his family as refugees, but that is what they were — fleeing their home for an insecure future in a foreign land.

Wonderful Counselor, Everlasting God, Almighty Father, Prince of Peace. Oh, and refugee. Our Savior became Refugee Jesus. The other savior wanted to kill him.

You can find a striking depiction of the flight into Egypt, as it is called by Giovanni Battista Tiepolo, drawn with pen and brown ink with brown wash over black chalk. (Look up these paintings on your smartphone or tablet while I'm talking if you want to really see them come to life.) Instead of traversing the typical desert landscape, the family is crossing a body of water in a boat like those used in the artist's native Venice. There's a boatman standing in the prow hurriedly pushing away from the shore. Mary, holding the infant Jesus, is entering the boat, with Joseph huddled below. An angel hovers over the family, perhaps calming Mary, as the family flees Herod's soldiers. Does Mary see the angel? She seems calm. I wonder if this is the same angel Joseph listened to in his dreams? Joseph heard God speaking through an angel, listened to the warning, and acted. Have you ever felt you were receiving an urgent message from God? How did you respond? What happened? Speak to me, God. I'll try hard to listen.

Why Egypt? Long before, the prophet Jeremiah warned the people against fleeing to Egypt, even though they faced the destruction of their nation and temple under the armed might of the Babylonians (Jeremiah 41:17, 42, and following). He reminded them that they had been slaves in Egypt. Egypt was the enemy.

But the fact is that some of God's people not only went to Egypt, they thrived. Many of them became mercenaries, fighting for the Persians who were occupying Egypt. They lived on an island on the Nile River called Elephantine. Some lived in Alexandria and became philosophers. They stayed, and they prospered.

No doubt Joseph knew about colonies of Jewish people scattered throughout Egypt. He sought one out. They had somewhere to go. We don't know where. As a refugee family Joseph, Mary, and Jesus no doubt found themselves among fellow Jews in Egypt, but even so, they were not at all like the people they knew in Judea. Their Bethlehem accents and customs made them outsiders. People celebrated the great holidays, like Passover, very differently.

From the very beginning Jesus knew what it meant to be a stranger in a strange land. Then, having grown up speaking with an "Egyptian" accent, he moved with his family, bypassing Bethlehem because there was another Herod who ruled, and moving to Galilee where he was probably mocked for speaking with an accent.

I think Jesus may have never fit in anywhere. With different accents, using different words, getting used to different customs, you have to ask, did he ever fit in, even as an adult, in Nazareth? Remember when he later preached in his hometown of Nazareth some questioned his identity. Who is this man? Isn't he the carpenter's son? He was rejected in his home town by his own people.

Part of what it meant for Jesus to become our Savior is that he shared our own restlessness, that comes from realizing we don't have a home in this world anymore. Isaiah said this when he proclaimed "...he became their savior in all their distress. It was no messenger or angel but his presence that saved them." (Isaiah 63:8-9).

He became their savior in all their distress.

He became their savior in all his distress.

He became their savior because of his distress.

He knows.

I hear the child Jesus, roused by his father and mother, being told they are going to leave Bethlehem and they aren't coming back, asking:

"Why are we leaving in the middle of the night?

"Can we take my stuff?

"When will we see my grandparents again?

"What will people be like in the place where we are going?"

I see the child Jesus struggling because his accent is different than the Egyptian Jewish children. I see Jesus struggling when they move up to Galilee after the death of Herod the Great, living in Nazareth, where the other children tell him he talks funny.

And I see why it was important, as Isaiah said, that God did not send an angel or messenger. As Isaiah said, "...his presence saved them. His love, pity lifted them up" (Isaiah 63:9). Jesus understands our sorrows because Jesus shares them.

Which Savior do you want? How about the one who knows us? Who has been where we have been?

Our distress is God's distress. God's solution was to come down and dwell with us and share our afflictions — including that of the refugee. The refugee Jesus is an essential part of who he is. He is a stranger in a strange land. There were Jews in Egypt, He was among his own. Yet they were not at all like his own.

Most of us don't think of Jesus and his family as refugees, but that's what they were — fleeing their home for an insecure future in a foreign land. Those who have been forced to abandon their homes and possessions — either permanently or temporarily — may find solace in learning that Jesus and his parents knew the refugee experience firsthand. Matthew told us that Jesus is Immanuel, 'God-With-Us.' God is with refugees. For the rest of us . . . what shall we do? Most of us have no personal experience as refugees. But did your ancestors come to the United States because they were escaping war or looking for work, and so were political or economic refugees? It's likely that many of them came without any sort of official papers because, for much of our history, one simply arrived. Stop for a moment and reflect upon your family's history and journey. May the refugee Jesus inspire us so that as we have been received, we may receive others.

The great building achievements and wealth of the one savior came at the expense of the people he ruled. As for his works, his gardens even the temple, whose magnificent stones caused all — including the apostles — to stare in open-mouthed wonder, they would come to nothing. His statues were melted down. Only the stone pedestals remain.

But we can share in the living legacy of our Savior, Jesus. This season beckons with light and hope. Let us share this light, this hope, with those who share the condition of Jesus as refugee, as outsider, as one who does not fit in for any variety of reasons. Let us share their distress as God has shared ours in the living presence of Emmanuel, God with us, Jesus, man of sorrows, Son of God.

New Year's Day
Matthew 25:31-46

Now! Now!

Happy New Year! Today is the start of a new year, a time of fresh starts, resolutions, new beginnings, and renewed hope. In popular art we depict the old year as a decrepit old man walking off the stage, and the new year as an infant full of promise.

But, there is nothing intrinsically new or yearly about January 1. History, chance, and custom have made this the first day of the year to our way of thinking, but there are many other New Year Days celebrated around the world, both in the past and the present. In the Jewish Calendar, for instance, the New Year's holiday is celebrated in the fall. It is called Rosh Hashanah. But in the Old Testament our Jewish cousins also celebrated the New Year in the spring, with Passover.

In Shakespeare's day the new year began on the first day of spring, which in those days was celebrated on March 25. March 24 might be 1592, but the next day would be 1593.

If you're a regular at a Chinese restaurant, you can't help but notice the posters celebrating the Chinese New Year some time in February or March, wherever it falls in that particular year.

In a way, how we mark time and when we celebrate the new year is immaterial. And while resolutions for self-improvement are worthy goals, the greatest satisfaction is resolving on New Year's Day to becoming the healing presence of Jesus in a suffering world.

When it comes to the church calendar, the new year began with the First Sunday of Advent. We're still in the Christmas season, with six days left to go until the Feast of the Epiphany that celebrates the arrival of the Magi. But let's be honest. Most of us have had it with Christmas and after today's feasting and football we're ready to say goodbye to all of it. Most of us ate too many Christmas cookies, cakes, pies, and other assorted treats. Most of us say we're sick of the sight of all those sweets and there's no way we could eat another chocolate covered cherry, but deep inside we know it's not true and that's why we're ready on January 2 to buckle down, buy a gym membership, join a weight loss program, or embark on some other New Year's resolution, even if it's something like reading the *Collected Works of Charles Dickens*.

Speaking of Dickens, it's likely that at some point during this past month you saw one of the many filmed adaptions of one of his most memorable stories — *A Christmas Carol*. You know what I'm talking about — the story of the miser Ebenezer Scrooge, who is visited by the ghost of his partner Marley who warns him that he will that night be visited by the ghosts of Christmas Past, Present, and Future. Marley shows him a ghastly sight — the fate suffered by many callous souls, which awaits Scrooge if he does not reform. Marley opens the curtain onto a scene of condemned spirits who suffer no physical torments in their damnation. Instead, their punishment is they must witness scenes of horrifying suffering by the poor, without being able to do anything to help. In life these individuals ignored the need all around them. In death they regret eternally everything they failed to do. Fortunately, Scrooge is changed by these encounters and opens his heart — and wallet — to aid those suffering in his midst.

A few decades later, this same theme was explored with a little more humor by H.H. Munro, who wrote under the name Saki, in his short story "Filboid Studge." In that story, a minor clerk dreams up an advertising campaign for Pipenta, a dismal breakfast cereal that has failed. He renames it Filboid Studge, and his only advertising consists of a poster showing the demons in hell torturing the damned (many of whom are recognizable as celebrities of that age) by holding the breakfast food just out of their reach. Underneath the scene is written, "They cannot buy it now." The cereal became an overnight sensation.

Both scenes demonstrated an essential element of today's passage from Matthew — though we have no idea when it might occur, at some point we will no longer be able to serve Jesus and the people of the world. There is a literal deadline for all of us, after which the gospel suggests we will regret what we have left undone for the kingdom — and for Jesus.

Today's reading from Matthew is about the end of the world, and it is the only time in the gospels where we see Jesus standing in the last judgment. And who hasn't thought about what that will be like?

I am reminded of one of the old Dunkers, part of the plain folk of Pennsylvania. His name was Israel Poulson Sr., (1770-1856), but he was cast from a different mold than his fellow sober-sided brethren. Most Dunkers were Germanic, but Israel, who was half Native-American, was abandoned at the age of seven then adopted and raised in a Dunker family. Dunkers renounced musical instruments and sang their hymns acapella, in German. Israel preached in English and played the fiddle. He was not only a fence-mender when it came to his ministry, he also built actual fences, smoked a pipe, and despite what Jesus said about them, was proud to be a tax collector. He also made a special point of encouraging women to enter the ministry.

He was famous as a story teller. One of his stories, titled "The Loaf of Bread," concerned a vision of the last judgment, in which "an immense concourse of people" slowly pressed forward to a set of giant scales. Their good deeds were on one side, and for many their good deeds were not enough to shift the balance in their favor. According to his story, when he stepped on the scales:

For an instant he seemed to hold his own, then he could feel himself slowly but surely rising. "Weighed and found wanting." He was just being condemned, when the judge was halted by someone running in the distance, frantically waving his hand, and calling at the top of his voice. It was a boy who held something under his arm. On he came, pushing fiercely through the crowd as fast as he could. The judge waited. The boy forced himself under the scales. Taking what was under his arm, in both hands, he gave it a toss up into the scale in which Brother Poulson was standing. Down came the scale in balance. 'Accepted," pronounced the judge. Brother Poulson looked down at his feet. There lay a loaf of bread. He recognized it as the loaf he had once given to a poor widow. (From *History of the Church of the Brethren of the Eastern District of Pennsylvania, 1708-1915*, p. 200)

Now just for a little context, the passage we read earlier in Matthew 25 is actually the third upon this theme of judgment. In the first, Jesus told a parable about five bridesmaids that made sure they had flasks of oil for their lamps, anticipating the unexpected yet always impending arrival of the bridegroom. Five others did not. The latter five were refused admission to the wedding celebrations.

In the second section, Jesus told about a man about to go on an extended trip, that put his three slaves in charge of five, three, and one talents, respectively. A talent was a huge sum of money. The first two invested their money, always a risky venture, but it paid off when they doubled what they were given, and were received into their master's joy. The third, fearful of judgment, buried the money, returned it intact without any loss or any gain, and for his lack of initiative he was cast out into the darkness.

This scene of judgment, like the two parables that preceded it, showed the response of Jesus not to lack of faith, but failure to act on that faith.

There are three very dramatic touches you might have missed in this passage. First, even though this is a series of three stories, only the first two are parables. The first two were apocalyptic in tone, looking toward the end times and advising one to be ready. This third is apocalypse itself. It's too late to prepare. It was too late for the characters described. It is not too late for us, if we pay attention.

Second, there is a dramatic revelation, a pulling away of a mask and costume. The Son of Man is an ambiguous term. God described Ezekiel as the "son of earth" or "son of man" over ninety times, recalling our humble origins from the dust. Ezekiel was simply a human being caught up in extraordinary events. That's all the term really means.

The prophet Daniel spoke of seeing one "like a son of man" who approached the throne of the Ancient of Days, who was given dominion over all peoples, forever. There is a transition from a figure of earth elevated to become a figure of glory and power.

In this story, the Son of Man, the son of earth, spoke as king! The mask was fully pulled away. Jesus, the humble man of sorrows, who had no place to lay his head, who would die naked on a cross, is back, and you have done what you have done or you have not done what you have not done, and it's time to add up the final scores and find out just where you stand.

Finally, there's an interesting word used when those who have failed ask the king, "Lord, when was it that we saw you hungry or thirsty or a stranger or naked or sick or in prison, and did not take care of you?" (Matthew 25:44).

The Greek word translated "take care" is based on *diakonos,* a word sometimes translated as "deacon," and in some churches denoting a specific rank or office. But what it really means is table waiter, someone willing to do the gutty work that to be done so folks can be served. In Luke, Martha impatiently asked Jesus to tell her sister Mary to lend a hand putting dinner on the table, "Is it nothing to you that my sister is leaving me alone to *deacon*?" (Luke 10:40). Waiting tables, serving up food, to Jesus, and to the least of these who stand in his place, is an extraordinarily powerful symbol of what it means to be God's people.

What is astounding here was that Jesus did not line up everyone and ask if they had accepted him as Lord and Savior. He did not quiz them on their communion or liturgical practices. There was no mention of who chaired the altar flower committee, or any of the other things that sometimes seem so important to us in churches. Instead, the dichotomy is pretty simple. If you fed the hungry, clothed the naked, welcomed the stranger, gave drink to the thirsty, visited the sick or those in prison, or any of the least of these, you served Jesus, and you're in. If not, you didn't, and you're out.

This is what Christian history has been heading toward all along. The reign of Christ is one of compassion, of practicality, of doing. The accounting, the reckoning, the judgment, is about serving not only each other, but those on the margins, the untouchables, even those on the wrong side of the law.

And what happens in these stories — the foolish bridesmaids miss out on the wedding they were waiting for. The timid servant misses out on the joy of his master. And those who failed to serve the least of these missed out — forever.

As I mentioned earlier, New Year's Day is not Epiphany, but this is the time of year we remember the Magi. They weren't believers in the one God. They were following a sign, though they weren't sure what it might lead to. They just knew that the signs showed that a king was born and they went to bring gifts. They served the king.

You're one up on the Magi. You know exactly who they were seeking. You know where his journey led. You know it didn't end on the cross. You know because he lives we too will live.

Let's close with two basic truths. This year won't be like any other year. This year will be like every other year. Jesus Christ is the same, yesterday, today, and tomorrow. That means it is always time to act.

There is only one resolution worth making this year — the same thing we should resolve every year — to serve Jesus, visibly, actively, wholeheartedly, while we have time. Do it while we're still here — while we can make a difference, on behalf of Jesus, for God's world, in God's kingdom.

Amen.

Second Sunday After Christmas Day
John 1:(1-9) 10-18

Walk Like An Egyptian

The size, scale, and mystery of Ancient Egypt fascinated all of Europe during the eighteenth and nineteenth centuries. What made Egypt all the more mysterious were the indecipherable hieroglyphics (Greek for "writing of the gods") that covered the walls and towers of this lost civilization.

What did they say? Some felt they would never be deciphered because the Egyptians had solved all the ancient mysteries of existence, so these symbols were encoded with spiritual revelations that probed the depths of eternal truth, beyond the understanding of those who followed.

Then, in 1799, while Napoleon was busy conquering Egypt on his way to planned world domination, a black stone was unearthed at a fort in Rashid (Rosetta to the French) and shortly thereafter a lieutenant realized what a find had been discovered! This Rosetta Stone, as it came to be known, displayed a royal decree in three languages — hieroglyphics, an Egyptian language known as Demotic, and Greek.

In those days, any schoolboy worth his salt learned Greek. With the Greek as a guide it should be easy to translate the hieroglyphics. Soon, all of the Egyptian wisdom would be open to the western world. Right?

Well, it wasn't that simple, and part of the problem was that experts were convinced that the hieroglyphics expressed great ideas, not letters and sounds.

Politics intervened. The English drove the French out of Egypt and moved the Rosetta Stone to England as a spoil of war. This set off a Cold War combat of sorts between an Englishman, Thomas Young, and a Frenchman, Jean-François Champollion, to decode hieroglyphics.

Young, a polymath and the great scientist of his age, had the first great insight. Surely the names of the rulers mentioned in the Greek would have to be translated with symbols that stood for sound. There were certain groups of symbols surrounded by ovals. As it turned out, he was right: the symbols in those ovals sounded out royal names. But he still thought most hieroglyphics were symbols, and not letters representing sounds.

Champollion, a much younger but sickly man, thought of nothing but Egyptology. He was puzzled by a reference in an ancient Greek document that connected the Egyptian words "duck" with "sun," and "mother" with "vulture." He then had the insight — some hieroglyphics were pictures. Some stood for sounds. Some were "rebuses," pictures that sounded like certain words, as in our language where the picture of an eye can stand for "I", while a bee sounds like "be."

There was a picture of a duck with a circular sun next to it. Champollion realized that it was referring to a Pharoah's title! In ancient Egyptian the word "duck" sounded like "son," and each pharaoh was the son of the sun!

The mystery was solved! Hieroglyphics turned out to be a lot like other languages, which developed from pictures to symbols to letters, and kept traces of all three.

In Greek, as in ancient Egyptian, some words stand for several things. They can create a picture in our mind, like a duck, but also stand for deep theological truths!

In the same way there's one word from the gospel of John that calls to mind a concrete and practical everyday image but helps us decode the real meaning and mystery of the Incarnation, the appearance of God in human form that is at the center of the good news John proclaimed.

The first chapter of John's gospel was the opposite of hieroglyphics. There seemed to be no mystery at all. The gospel of John has the simplest vocabulary in the New Testament probably because Greek was John's second language. Yet that is deceptive, because this simple Greek contains layer after layer of meaning.

In the first chapter, John told us the story of Jesus as the Word, *logos,* from which we get our word logo, as in advertising symbols that tell you everything you want to know about a product at a glance. People are excited about logos. They wear logos, whether it's a clothing brand, a symbol for an athletic team, the mascot for their school, to share something basic about their identity. The logo for one prominent sportswear company consists of a swoosh, kind of like a hieroglyphic that suggests graceful speed.

Jesus being identified as the Word at the beginning of creation deliberately alluded to Genesis 1:1, where God spoke a word and things came into being. It also calls to mind Proverbs 8, where the living words are the words of wisdom, spoken by a mom in the marketplace to wayward children, calling them — us really — back to common sense and good living. Wisdom makes the same claim as the logos, to be present at the beginning. Jesus is the Word of creation, the Word of wisdom, Emmanuel, God with us!

But Word is not the word I'm thinking of.

One of the first words God speaks in Genesis is "light!" as in "Let there be light, and there was light." In recent decades we have banished the night, lost the stars, because we have abused the gift of light, but in previous millennia light in the darkness brought safety, security, and hope. The first thing that happened in Genesis was God's Spirit hovering over the face of the deeps, keeping chaos in the form of ancient gods named Formless and Void, before the light God created kept the power of darkness at bay. In John's gospel we discover that in the word is light, and the light shined in the darkness, and the darkness could not overcome it. We learn that Jesus is the true light, the one coming into the world.

But light is not the word I'm thinking of either.

No, the word I am thinking of is found in John 1:14 — "The Word became flesh and dwelt among us." But the word translated as "dwelt" has as its root *skene,* which describes a particular way of dwelling among us: a tent.

Tents were made from animal skins. See how we get the word "skin" from "skene"? So the word became flesh and "tented" among us. Unlike Moses who was raised in Pharaoh's household, Jesus was born to a teenager in a Palestinian village on the edge of Roman Empire. When God became human, God tented, or roughed it.

Since "skene" can mean tent, it also reminds us of the tent that was the home of that most holy ark of the covenant, which traveled with the people through the desert. When they were starving, thirsting, complaining, God tented with them. When King David wanted to build a mighty temple, God through the prophet Nathan reminded David that a tent had always been good enough.

"Skene" is also the source for the theatrical word "scene." The "skene," made out of animal skins, was the word for the scenic painted backdrop in Greek drama. Jesus is part of a great scene, a tragedy and catastrophe with a happy ending.

If I were translating this verse, I would say, "The Word was made flesh and camped among us." Or maybe, "The Word was made flesh and roughed it among us!"

Skin, scene, tent, roughing it — *skene* is the word that serves several functions in the good news of Jesus Christ. In a way, it tells me everything I need to know about Jesus!

A big moment in the gospels came when people recognized Jesus for who he was. The disciples had seen Jesus heal the sick and raise the dead. They had seen the lives of a Samaritan village change because an outsider, the woman who had five husbands and was now living with a man outside of marriage, recognized Jesus as the living water and the Word of God. They saw Jesus weep at the tomb of his good friend Lazarus and call him forth from the tomb.

And they saw the Word made flesh gird himself with a towel and descend to a knee to wash their feet when they gathered together to eat. He who was proclaimed the Lamb of God by John, the one who had come to take away the sin of the world, did something unprecedented in ancient history. Nowhere before Jesus can we find an example of where a superior washes the feet of one below their station. Indeed, washing feet is a task given to slaves who cannot refuse the assignment. Peter was so alarmed he insisted he would have none of it, but Jesus replied that if he was not willing to have his feet washed they would have no part in each other. Indeed, Jesus told all of us that we are to follow his example, not only in literally washing each other's feet, but in being prepared to perform the grittiest tasks for each other so that Jesus becomes incarnate in our midst again.

This is why the Apostle Paul said, in words that seem to call to mind the feet washing, "Let the same mind be in your that was in Christ Jesus, who, though he was in the form of God, did not regard equality with God as something to be exploited, but emptied himself, taking the form of a slave, being born in human likeness, and being found in human form, he humbled himself and became obedient to the point of death, even death on a cross," (Philippians 2: 5-8). It is this that elevates the name of Jesus, we are told, so that "at the name of Jesus every knee should bend" (Philippians 2:10) just as he bent his knee in obedient service.

Skin. Scene. Tent. Roughing it.

Where do we find Peter, before he is led by the Holy Spirit to the house of Cornelius the centurion, where he baptized the entire Gentile household into the family of God? We find him at the home of Simon the tanner. Tanners cured and processed animal skins, necessary for tents. Theirs was a smelly job that was considered unclean by some because they dealt with dead animals. But Peter chose to live with a tanner, no matter what others thought, though it meant in the eyes of some that he too was unclean, and it was through this humility that he was ready to open the doors of the New Testament church to all.

Skin. Scene. Tent.

The apostle Paul spent eighteen months in Corinth, roughing it, tenting it, and working with two other tentmakers among the Corinthian house churches. He did not come as a tourist, or an honored guest, but as a hard worker. Corinth was relatively rich compared to other cities in the Greek peninsula. That's because it was located on the strip of land, known as an isthmus, that connected Greece to the mainland of Europe. Ships crossing the Mediterranean would eliminate some of the risk connected with commerce on the sea by either stopping at Corinth, shipping their boats by wheel across the few miles of the isthmus, or unloading a larger boat entirely and shipping the goods overland to a waiting boat. Either way this meant that a lot of people from different ethnic and religious backgrounds from across the empire came to this place to take part in making money by moving goods from one spot to another without actually manufacturing anything. Those who traveled there needed tents, or needed their tents repaired. Paul and his friends proved this needed service, demonstrating that followers of Jesus also share in the economy of life.

Corinth was also the center for the Corinthian games, which were held in between Olympic years. Paul served those people too. We as Christians are not absent from the economy but actively involved with people of all backgrounds. And we rough it, we tent it, making it possible for the world to see Christians as an essential element across the globe.

Skin. Scene. Tent.

How important is it to rough it? Moses found out. He was raised in comfort in Pharaoh's household, but when as an adult he saw an Egyptian overseer beating one of the Hebrew slaves, he intervened, he killed the Egyptian and hid the body. However, when he attempted to stop a fight the next day involving two Hebrews, and after breaking it up one of the two said, "Who made you a ruler and judge over us?" (Exodus 2:14). Moses realized no one respected him because of the way he was raised, and he fled into the desert. It was only after a sojourn in the wilderness and a commission from God in the burning bush that he had the street credentials to be their leader.

There's no faking it. A story is told about Tsar Peter the Great, who wanted to visit his people in disguise to see what life was like for them. He therefore travelled across Russia as a simple lieutenant. Or maybe not so simple. This lieutenant traveled in great luxury about his train, attended by many servants and an armed guard, and fake villages were created in advance of his arrival, and the people coached to show proper respect to a simple lieutenant, so that he could go back home thinking all was well.

Jesus, by contrast, lamented that birds have nests and foxes have dens, but he had no place to lay his head. Only at the Transfiguration was he revealed as the true light of the world, attended upon by Moses and Elijah, with a testimony from a divine voice speaking from the heavens. Otherwise, people felt free to curse him, to threaten him, and eventually to beat him senseless, crown him with thorns, cast lots for his clothes and nail him to a cross.

This is the scenic backdrop to the great drama of the Word coming into the world.

Skin. Scene. Tent.

There's an old folk hymn that, according to the story, was sung by an Appalachian girl in North Carolina and transcribed by folklorist John Jacob Niles (in the public domain): *I wonder as I wander out under the sky*

How Jesus my Savior did come for to die
For poor on'ry people like you and like I
I wonder as I wander out under the sky...."

Jesus camped among us. Jesus tented among us poor ornery people. And we are called to do the same. Whether in organized disaster relief or simply bringing relief to a neighbor in the form of a casserole, we are called to be campers, roughing it, not tourists at a zoo, pointing at all the people on display.

Think of how God has roughed it with you, during the tough stretches of your life. Reflect on your life's drama. What kind of play has your life been? When you do think God make an entrance?

A lot of images are called up by this one word, *skene,* one symbol that stands for so much. Maybe we can say "Everything we needed to know about the good news of Jesus Christ we learned from one word."

Skene. Skin. Scene. Tent.

Jesus.

Amen.

(Want to know more? See *The Writing of the Gods: The Race To Decode the Rosetta Stone,* by Edward Dolnick, Scribner, 2021, and *The Rosetta Stone and the Rebirth of Ancient Egypt,* by John Ray, Harvard University Press, 2007.)

I've Got A Bad Feeling About This

It's one of the most famous recurring lines in film history. In 1977, in the movie then called *Star Wars*, Luke Skywalker looked with awe as the Millennium Falcon approached the Death Star, and said, "I have a very bad feeling about this." A little later in the film, as our heroes spill into a Galactic Trash Bin, Han Solo muttered, "I got a bad feeling about this." A moment later the walls of the trash compactor begin to close in on them.

The line became a running gag. In all eleven *Star Wars* movies one or another of the characters says a variation of that line. In *Rogue One*, the robot K-2SO starts to say, "I've got a bad feeling about th---" when he's silenced by Cassian. The greatest variation comes when the young Han Solo enthused, "I have a really good feeling about this!" in the movie *Solo: A Star Wars Story*, before an especially desperate maneuver.

And although most fans did not catch it the first time they saw it, in the penultimate movie, *The Last Jedi*, the droid BB-8 said, "I have a bad feeling about this," but it's in a series of binary tweets. We humans may not have understood him, but the other characters did. Poe Dameron gently scolded, "Happy beeps, buddy! Happy beeps!" while Princess Leia responded by saying, "Just for the record Commander Dameron, I'm with the droid on this one."

All this is prelude to my statement that when the Magi came on scene in the second chapter of Matthew I feel like repeating that famous line, "I've got a bad feeling about this."

And so should you.

But we don't. We have a good feeling whenever we see the entrance of the Magi in a Christmas pageant. Kids love to be one of the kings. They get to wear a robe, and a crown, and carry a box with a gift. One of the gifts they understand. Everyone understands gold. Frankincense? Myrrh? Not so much, but who cares? And who doesn't look forward to singing "We Three Kings" this time of the year?

First of all, let's set the record straight. They were not kings. The confusion comes from preachers and painters centuries later, who interpreted verses from Isaiah 60, speaking about the restoration of hope to the defeated Israelites, to refer to the Magi. It's an understandable confusion. In the third verse of that chapter Isaiah said, "Nations will come to your light and kings to the brightness of your dawn." Three verses later there's a reference to camels, gold, and frankincense. Two of the three gifts and the word kings. What's a good interpreter supposed to think?

But Matthew didn't talk about kings. He used the word "magi," often translated in the New Testament as "wise men." However, the Greek word *Magi* is a pejorative term, an insult, that should be translated "magician," "astrologer," or "sorcerer!" And sorcerers don't come out looking too good in the Bible.

The evil Simon Magus (the singular of magi) believed the Holy Spirit, like secret cosmic knowledge, could be bought for a price (Acts 8:9-24). In Ephesus, Magi opposed Paul's ministry because a treasure trove of magic books, worth 165 years' worth of daily wages, were destroyed publicly by converts to Christianity (Acts 19:18-20).

One of the most memorable scenes from the Old Testament involved the witch of Endor (Yikes! A *Star Wars* allusion in the Hebrew scriptures?) who the embattled King Saul commanded to conjure up the spirit of the dead prophet Samuel, who then condemned Saul for this act (see 1 Samuel 28:3-25). There are many warnings in the Hebrew scriptures, such as the one in Leviticus 19:31 — "Do not turn to mediums or wizards; do not seek them out, to be defiled by them: I am the Lord your God." And Exodus 22:18 is clear: "You shall not permit a female sorcerer to live."

So both the Hebrew scriptures and the Greek New Testament warn us against those who practice magic. We *should* have a very bad feeling about all of this.

That's why, when the Magi took the stage, Matthew drew our attention to this. This was a big deal. Matthew's first word in the chapter was *idou*, usually translated "Behold!" which really means: "Look out!" Magi! "Warning! Warning!" Pay attention.

What will happen when these magicians team up with the worst king ever? King Herod, who ruled the region on behalf of the Romans, was admired by the rich and the powerful in the empire because of his elaborate building projects, innovative gardens, who became the savior of the Olympics of 12 BC by bailing them out financially when much of the western world was facing bankruptcy because of a ruinous series of wars.

But he was hated by his own people. He taxed them heavily, perpetrated atrocities, and was so paranoid he killed many of his relatives for fear they would overthrow him.

We have every reason to wonder — what happens when you mix Magi and Herod? Do you get a league of super villains? What kind of reign of terror ensues when sorcerers team up with the evil king?

That's why I like "sorcerers" as a translation, because it highlights the turnaround here. The sorcerers in Matthew's gospel (like the Samaritan in Jesus' parable as told in Luke) confounded conventional wisdom by acting righteously. They turned out to be the bulwark between Herod and Jesus. They played a part in saving his life!

While a star may have pointed them in the right direction, scripture got them to their final destination. " 'Where is the child who has been born king of the Jews? For we observed his star at its rising, and have come to pay him homage" (v. 2). The Magi interpreted these signs to mean a king would be born in Judea!

The logical thing to do was to go to the political center of Judea, Jerusalem, and ask for directions. King Herod, frightened that divine forces may conspire to replace him — and if King Herod was afraid everybody better be afraid — asked his religious experts if the scriptures gave a roadmap to this newborn king. They determined that a verse from Micah, originally delivered to assure God's people that a king like David would come from Bethlehem and protect them against the nation-devouring

Assyrians, could be re-interpreted to mean God was sending another shepherd-king to bring peace and security.

Notice that everyone in the court heard the scripture, but only the sorcerers traveled the five miles to see for themselves! No matter how tired you get this season, don't let it prevent you from traveling a few feet to admire the artwork of children, to listen to their wisdom, to bake cookies together, or to answer questions.

Herod and his court missed the sign completely, and not just because they weren't stargazers. The courtiers weren't ready for any sign of God that might threaten their paranoid king. The Magi were looking for a sign, and were ready—if they saw one—to pack and go! The Magi saw, and acted.

They brought gifts of gold, frankincense, and myrrh. These may seem like strange gifts but they may have been handier than you think for the young family of Joseph, Mary, and Jesus. Joseph is described elsewhere in the gospels as a "tekton," often translated as carpenter, but which really meant, "jack of all trades," someone who could build or fix anything. That certainly meant that Joseph could provide a steady living for his family, but when it became necessary to suddenly relocate to Egypt that gold could have helped their travel expenses and help to replace tools and equipment that they might have left behind in their haste.

Frankincense would have improved the quality of life because people valued good smells in those days, in contrast to our era where we try to eliminate as many smells as possible. Potential customers might have assumed from the frankincense that Joseph and Mary were successful people of substance, and supported this new jack of all trades when he relocated to Egypt.

And myrrh reminded everyone that we don't live forever. It was a perfume associated with the preparation of bodies for burial. Knowing we won't live forever can be a spur to live as much as possible in the moment.

So the sorcerers, who should have represented evil in this scene, turn out to be the most helpful to the new family, and in the process fulfill one of the themes of the prophets from of old, that one day all the nations of the earth would come together to worship the Lord. The people are to prepare for this great day.

It was not just the sorcerers. In the Hebrew scriptures the Persian emperor, who worshiped another god, was described as the Lord's great servant when he called for the return of God's people to their land, to rebuilt the temple and restore hope. In the gospel of John the outsider, the Samaritan woman, who was part of a nation at odds with God's people, and who was an outcast in her Samaritan village because she had had five husbands and was living with a sixth man, was the evangelist who brought the whole village into the fold.

The feast of the Epiphany celebrates the light shining for everyone in the world. It's not just our light, any more than the faith belonged to Herod just because he finished the building of the great temple of Solomon. The faith is for the people we least expect. The light shines *from* everybody, not just *for* everybody.

Part of what this story demonstrates is that the outsiders, the Magi, are open to the leading of the Holy Spirit when good church folks have got their hearts closed. Matthew's first two chapters demonstrate the leading of God's Spirit through a series of dreams. Joseph is the recipient of most of those dreams. In the first dream, he listens to the angel who tells him to marry Mary, despite the fact that she is pregnant even though they were engaged. Joseph will also listen to the angel in the dream and flee Bethlehem for Egypt when told Herod desires to kill Jesus. He also responds to the dream that tells him it is safe to go back.

Part of that series of dreams includes one given to the Magi themselves, warning them not to go back to Herod to report where Jesus could be found, as he had asked. They are to go home another way. If Joseph proves himself righteous by listening to the dream dispelling doubt about Mary's pregnancy, and responding immediately to the dream telling him to flee with his family, so too the Magi also are part of this great chain, not only by responding to the celestial signs, but listening to the dream and going home by another route.

God used the sorcerers, the Magi, as part of the great plan to bring light into the world. Does that mean that astrology is all right? I don't think so. In AD 115, Ignatius, the overseer of the Christians of Antioch, wrote about the star to the Ephesian Christians as he was being shipped to Rome to be thrown to the wild beasts for refusing to deny Christ. Ignatius tells the believers in Ephesus that certain beliefs have been hidden, but Christ has been revealed in this way: "One star in the heavens outshone all the other stars, and its light, beyond words, and its foreignness astounded all the rest, so that a chorus of stars, together with the sun and the moon gathered around it. So much greater was its light that they were puzzled — what was this new thing so unlike everything else? This was how magic and fear were outshone, ignorance washed away, and the old kingdom was destroyed, for God was revealed in a human to reveal the newness of life eternal. Everything was changed because the plan was for death to be dissolved." (*author's translation*)

When the Magi came, following the star, looking for the new king, it was the beginning of something new. Theirs was a long and complicated journey and there were preparations to be made. We too must prepare for a journey. Whether it's the trip to the Galilean home, home devotions with the Upper Room, a big vacation, or the trip to our eternal home, we all need to prepare in advance to get the most out of each trip! The holidays are over, and now we're preparing for ordinary time, real life, normalcy, or as close to normalcy as we're going to get.

Everything was changed! We live. We learn. We grow. God uses us whether we're ready or not, whether we fully understand yet or not. And this is all on the assumption that we can change. Over the course of my life as a Christian I hope I have conquered my own ignorance, and now see all people in God's light. As you too have grown, what have you learned? How have you changed? In what ways are you the same? Jesus, shine in our lives always. May we walk in the light of your life. May we too live, learn, grow, and change!

You know what? I've changed my mind. When the Magi walk on stage I've got a *good* feeling about this. That's because

God is demonstrating that the lost can not only be found, but they are as capable of listening to the Holy Spirit as the best of us, and not only that, they demonstrate that when the lost are saved, they too — and we too — can fulfill the will of the Lord.

Amen.

Headliners And Opening Acts

It's hard to believe now, but in 1963 the Beatles were listed last among a series of opening acts on a poster for a concert tour of England. Fresh from a grueling series of gigs at the Cavern Club in Hamburg, where the boys from Liverpool sharpened their performing skills, their manager looked for any venue that would draw the attention of their fellow Brits back their direction.

The headliner, a new pop star named Helen Shapiro was, as Ringo recalled, the only one who had a television in her dressing room, but she was, after all, the one everyone really came out to hear!

So John and Paul prepared for the future as they sat in the back of the bus traveling from town to town, writing new songs they hoped to sell to others.

But partway during the tour their early recordings became sudden hits. It wasn't long before fans were coming out specifically to hear the Beatles. They became the headliners. The other acts, famous in their time, slipped into the background, and were largely forgotten.

The last thing I want to do is get in trouble for comparing the Beatles to Jesus. Some people have forgotten, but at one point early in their career John Lennon made a rueful comment about Beatlemania, suggesting that to some of their fans the Beatles were bigger than Jesus. However it was meant, and the four mop tops were famous for their wicked sense of humor, the comment backfired, leading to a backlash in middle America. Many people took to burning their records. In the end, Lennon clarified his comments, saying that he wasn't saying it was a good thing that some people liked the Beatles more than Jesus — he was just making an observation.

It is helpful to think about this business of John the Baptist and Jesus as the headliner and the backup act. There's no question that at one point John the Baptist was the major headliner. Crowds came to the Jordan River to hear him. He wore a bizarre costume, calling to mind some of the ancient prophets with his strange clothes and strange actions. He ate locusts and honey. He challenged the high and mighty, mocking those who were powerful, drawing their ire, while delighting the ordinary people at the same time.

"You brood of vipers!" he called out, condemning the Pharisees and Sadducees who came to be baptized. "Who warned you to flee from the wrath to come." (Matthew 3:11)

Talk about a counter culture hero. I'm sure there was laughter when John challenged the rich and powerful. He was big! And though people may have looked over their shoulders in alarm when he made some of his comments, for the most part, at first at least, he got away with it!

Along the way he hinted that someone even more special would be taking his place. "I am not worthy to carry his sandals. He will baptize you with the Holy Spirit and fire." (Matthew 3:11)

Meanwhile, at the time Jesus was not even an opening act. Indeed, I wonder if Jesus really fit in anywhere. I've been mentioning in recent weeks how his background made Jesus something of an outsider. His mother was from Nazareth, but because of Joseph's connections with Bethlehem he was born there and spent his first couple of years near Jerusalem. He would have learned to speak there and had a Judean accent. Then, forced to flee to Egypt, he would have lived in a Jewish community somewhere in that region (and there were several), but people practiced the faith a little differently in different places, and he would grown up an outsider who began to speak like others, but among whom he didn't fit in.

And once again, after Herod's death that family moved not to Bethlehem, but because of fear about some of Herod's relations, they went north to Galilee and Nazareth. Once again, Jesus talked differently, and kids can be cruel about that. That's why I wonder if he ever fit in anywhere. Later he would be rejected at Nazareth. "Is this not the carpenter's son?" they ask (Matthew 13:54). Where could he have gotten this knowledge? His supposed hometown folks seem very puzzled about him.

Even with his cousin John seems puzzled about Jesus.

Yes, John the Baptist recognized Jesus as the one whose sandals he was not worthy to carry, but there doesn't seem to be any interaction that demonstrates they recognized each other as cousins. Granted, that is part of Luke's gospel, not Matthew's, but though Jesus eventually grew up in Galilee, he seems familiar with Jerusalem and Judea. He should have run into John regularly on those trips.

In such a close-knit culture familial relationships mattered a good deal. Luke told us the family travelled south every year to Jerusalem for Passover, and certainly that provided an opportunity for family to get together. But perhaps John, with much older parents, was orphaned sooner, and his paths did not often cross with that of Jesus.

So, with the great age difference between their mothers and a three-day-walk separating their two homes, perhaps the boy Jesus, as he grew up, had very little or even no contact with his cousin. Still, some of the questions John later asked of Jesus (see Matthew 11:3) when he as in prison make me wonder what exactly John knew about Jesus.

What was also intriguing was how when the main act had the chance to throw the spotlight on the up and coming star, he tried to decline the honor. John didn't want to baptize Jesus at first.

Some translate the phrase "John would have prevented him," in response to Jesus' request to be baptized, as "tried to hinder." John not only felt unqualified, it was as if he did not see this as God's plan.

But he did it anyway. His qualms, and the relationship between the families of John and Jesus didn't matter as much as their relationship within the kingdom of God.

Some might ask why Jesus had to be baptized, anyway? He was presented as sinless, and certainly not in need of a baptism of repentance. However, in this and many other things, Jesus showed his solidarity with us. He went through the same things as us, including a rite of humility.

Jesus himself said that this was done to fulfill all righteousness. Righteous and self-righteousness is not the same as what is meant by righteous. The righteousness of God is to be what we are meant to be. Like the old Shaker hymn says, " 'Tis the gift to be simple, 'tis the gift to be free, 'tis the gift to come down where we ought to be" (in the public domain). We all have roles to fulfill.

In colonial times the old German Baptists, one of the plain people often called the Dunkers, had a saying that they solemnly pronounced at the funeral of one of their members. "He filled his place." That meant simply that each one of us is called to fulfill a certain unique role that no one else can do, and it is by becoming the disciple Jesus created us to be that we best honor God in our life.

One thing is clear — God had a plan for John's life, and God has a plan for our lives. There's an Old Testament scripture from Isaiah that is often interpreted as referring to John the Baptist. Isaiah declared, "The Lord called me before I was born; while I was in my mother's womb he named me" (Isaiah 49:1).

So what is his place? What are we to make of John the Baptist, and what lesson should we take for ourselves from his life?

I think one way we can be like John the Baptist is to highlight and encourage the work of our fellow church members, not only the younger ones, and that is important, but also those who may be older but stepping into new avenues of service. More and more of us are exploring ministry in all its forms — youth ministry, pastoral ministry, counseling, and in many other ways — at a later period in our lives. We are bringing the skills and experience we have garnered in other avenues of life into this call from God.

There's a tendency to picture John as much older and wizened than Jesus, even though they were born within months of each other. And don't forget, life expectancy for many folks in their time was 25 to 35 years! Jesus was not a young man when at the age of thirty he was baptized and began to preach the coming of the kingdom of God. He had evidently taken Joseph's place, working as a carpenter, as the head of that family after his death.

There are many ways we can be John the Baptist. We need to shine the spotlight on those whom God is calling out to leadership in our congregation. After all, those rising to take our places need their time to run the show and shine!

And let us in turn be thankful for those who have been John the Baptist for us, for those who mentored us, called us forward, pointed us out, celebrated our talents, and led the way so we can become the disciples we are meant to be. It may even have been for something outside the realm of ministry. Some other couple perhaps gave us guidance by their example for how marriage really works, and how to really work at marriage. Sometimes we need an example for how to live with depression, or another chronic condition.

This is also true when it comes to divorce. If we have had to struggle through difficult times, we need to help others, especially because so many Christians are ready to clobber people with a few verses taken out of context. We need to show there is resurrection and new life after an old way of life dies, and that no one has to live in a toxic situation to please another's false gospel.

As cancer survivors, or cancer endurers, we can show that there is life in the desert, and in the midst of struggle, without knowing the outcome, God is present and we are present as well.

Just as John the Baptist's role was very limited, and he was soon off the stage, so too we can accept that sometimes we are very important in someone else's life, or they are important in ours, and then that time is over — and that's okay.

Because like any headliner who partway through the tour needs to step to the side so that the up and comer can take their place, John the Baptist knew when to get out of the way.

Everyone wants to be the headliner. Everyone wants to be the star. But the real stars are those who recognize there is only one headliner — and that is Jesus. When we try to put ourselves on the top of the billing we are setting ourselves up for a downfall. But when we give Jesus top billing, then our talents have a chance to shine.

John the Baptist provides a good example of this. He is the voice crying in the wilderness, bringing Isaiah's prophecy to life. He is the bridge between the Old and the New Testaments. He is Elijah, he is Malachi, he is Isaiah, but most of all, he is himself. He fills his place.

You know, later in the gospel, John, while wasting away in prison, sent a couple of his disciples to Jesus with some questions, and Jesus took those questions seriously and sent back an answer. He then reflected with the crowd about what John meant to him. "What did you go out into the wilderness to look at?" he asked. "A reed shaken by the wind? What did you go out to see? Someone dressed in soft robes?" (Matthew 11:7).

No, Jesus suggested what they came to see was a prophet. And as a prophet John was both the greatest and the least. This sounds like a paradox, a contradiction, but it's true for all of us as well. John died, but his work lives in Jesus. We are part of this great story that was begun before we ever stepped on the scene and because the power of Jesus will continue to change lives, and change the world, and redeem lost souls, because we played our part, as long as we keep Jesus at the center of all things. We are reeds, shaken by the wind, yet bouncing back, and enduring. And all eyes will continue to be directed to Jesus, the true headlining act, the one that matters, and that, after all, is what is most important.

Amen.

Second Sunday after the Epiphany
John 1:29-42

Seen And Unseen

The Hubble Space Telescope is being superseded by the Webb Space Telescope, but that groundbreaking instrument filled us with awe, opening up a window to the stars and causing us to gasp at the complexity of the universe God created. But as staggeringly beautiful we have found the cosmos to be, in some ways what we can't see is far more awe-inspiring.

Astronomer Vera Rubin (1928-2016) opened up the invisible to a world that refused to see it, and to be honest, her! Her deserved recognition was late in coming, mostly because she was a woman in what was once an almost exclusively male — and male chauvinist — field. While working at Palomar Observatory in the San Diego area, for instance, she was told there were no restrooms for women. So she cut out the silhouette of a figure wearing a skirt out of a sheet of paper and slapped it on the door of one of the men's bathrooms, and announced "There you go; now you have a ladies' room."

Though she had to overcome many obstacles, she eventually helped everyone see the unseeable.

Working with fellow astronomer Kent Ford she began to examine the Andromeda galaxy, a disklike galaxy that spins around and around like a record.

When was the last time you looked at a record on a record player? The next time you do, watch the outer edge and the inner ring of the record. They travel a different distance but they accomplish that at the same speed: thirty-three and third revolutions every minute.

Unlike a record, the conventional wisdom was that the distribution of stars in a galaxy would cause its outside edge to spin much more slowly than the inside. But Vera discovered the outer rim spun much, much faster than seemed possible, judging from the amount of matter astronomers observed.

It took a while for Rubin to have an "Aha!" moment, but she finally recalled that a couple of astronomers, Jan Oort in 1932 and Fritz Swicky in 1933, had once theorized that perhaps there was some sort of matter that was invisible that might explain certain discrepancies in predictions about the universe. Their theories had been dismissed because there was no proof that something like "dark matter" existed.

Since the outer reaches of the Andromeda Galaxy were spinning at a far faster rate than predicted, the best explanation, she decided, was there were huge amounts of this dark matter in the Andromeda Galaxy.

As with many breakthroughs, it took a while for the astronomical community to move from general dismissal of Rubin's theories (she was, after all, a woman) to total acceptance that her theory best explained what everyone was now observing. And that invisible dark matter has a tremendous effect on the history and future of the universe we *can* see.

One belief most people share in common is that we can't see God. Kids ask about that pretty early in the game once they begin to learn about God's existence. Where is God? Why can't we see God? How do we know God is there if God is invisible?

The ancients had no problem because they could see their god. Their gods might be immortal, and live on the top of some wonderful mountain, but they were always walking among people and could be seen in all sorts of forms if the god desired.

These people depicted their gods mostly in humanlike form. It might be an idealized human, but still, there were arms, legs, a face, and all that other stuff.

When you went into the temple of one of those ancient religions you'd see a statue representing the god. It would be awe-inspiring, colossal, bedecked in gold and jewels, but you could see it.

Things were different in the Jerusalem temple, built to honor the Lord, the God of Israel. The Ark of the Covenant included a throne, supported by angelic cherubim, but there was no visible figure to be seen seated there.

At one point Moses asked to see God, and was told that's not possible, that one cannot see God and live. Instead, God instructed Moses to hide in the cleft of a rock, while God walked by, and allowed him to see just the reflected glory.

Yet there are these odd moments in scripture. Jacob wrestled with "a man" all night. Later commentators identified this figure as an angel, but Jacob himself, permanently wounded from the encounter, would call the place Peniel, which means "face of God," because he had looked on the face of God and lived.

On the night before Joshua led his army seven times around the walls of Jericho, which would then come tumbling down, Joshua met up with a "man" who identified himself as the commander of the army of the Lord, which meant this person *is* the Lord.

And Moses, along with seventy elders, came face to face with God, and lived (Exodus 24:9ff).

In the New Testament the matter is made pretty clear: "No one has ever seen God. It is God the only Son, who is close to the Father's heart, who has made him known" (1 John 1:18).

If we're going to see God, John the Evangelist tells us in today's scripture reading, it will be through the Word, that mysterious unseen God, present at the creation, through whom all is created, and who, we learn in John 1:14, has made the invisible visible to us all.

And the Word became flesh and lived among us, and we have seen his glory, the glory as of a father's only son, full of grace and truth.

The Word is Jesus. At a time of God's choosing everything came together in creation so that the Word was made flesh. People saw Jesus and they understood God.

The gospel of John includes a number of signs by which people come to see Jesus and know God. The Samaritan woman at the well heard Jesus talk about the living water, and she got it. The blind man was not only given sight, but he saw clearly who Jesus was while the others argued about whether it was appropriate for the sign to take place. Mary and Martha were both deeply grieved that Jesus had not arrived in time to save their brother Lazarus from death, and yet they still proclaim their belief in the Word before Lazarus was called forth from the tomb. Nicodemus stood up for the crucified Jesus at great risk to himself because he finally got what it meant to be born again.

And Thomas, wrongly called Doubting Thomas, demonstrated why he was really believing Thomas because he proclaimed most clearly that the word was made flesh, and we could see God clearly in the one person who was both human and divine, addressing Jesus as "My Lord and my God!" (John 20:28). All these examples, all the words, were written "...so that you may come to believe that Jesus is the Messiah, the Son of God, and that through believing you may have life in his name" (John 20:31).

That settled it — kind of. Because even if we know we're looking at something invisible, the Word, made visible in Jesus, we may not recognize right away what it means, and why it's important for you, for me, for everyone, and every rock and pebble seen and unseen.

Fortunately one of the witnesses to the light, John who baptized Jesus, pointed Jesus out to some of the disciples and said these crucial words: "Here is the Lamb of God who takes away the sin of the world!" (1:29).

Something happened that was easy to miss! John announced the Lamb of God doesn't take away the *sins* of the world. You know, all the bad stuff we do which we need to repent and ask forgiveness for.

The Lamb of God takes away the *sin*, singular, of the world.

So what does that mean?

The sin of the world, singular, is no intertwined with everything — we can miss it. It might be invisible to us. But it's like a black hole. You can't see it but nothing escapes from it. The sin of the world is the evil we're all a part of, regardless of our good intentions. It's the sin we're all committing, just by being a part of each other.

Slavery, for instance. It's not something that just existed in the past. It's all around us, even in our own country. Things like sweat shops and sex slavery. People held in bondage by the powerful, producing products we buy. They may be manufactured here, or halfway around the world, and we may not know that we're taking part when we get a real bargain.

Churches don't want to admit that sexual abuse happens everywhere, including among their members, and they may refuse to see it, or admit it, and often churches want to wish it away, insisting it never happens in our midst.

There is silent suffering, depression, chronic illness, despair, and though we say we're always ready to help, sometimes people can't reach out anymore because everyone wants to fix things with this cure they've heard of or treatment that a cousin had, which means if it didn't work for the sufferer it must be their fault.

Finally, the chronically ill just get tired of talking about pain, because they're sure people are sick of them, so they sink out of our sight, but not God's sight.

Addiction is something that happens to other people in other churches. Not ours — we're too nice.

So the sin of the world is what Jesus came to take away, and in order to do it, we have to listen to God's prescription. Love, compassion, and endurance, are all necessary. Love especially, for as scripture reminds us: "No one has ever seen God; if we love one another, God lives in us, and his love is perfected in us" (1 John 4:12).

Seen and unseen — in the Gospel of John, Jesus saw the people others didn't notice. Like Nicodemus, who worried so much about what others thought that he visited Jesus under the cover of darkness — but he visited Jesus. And Jesus saw him.

Nobody saw the Samaritan woman because she went out to the well at midday when there was nobody there, not in the morning with the other women because she was so tired of being rejected. Jesus saw her, spoke to her, and treated her like a human being.

Nobody saw the man born in the ninth chapter of John as anything but the result of somebody's sin. They saw his disability, they didn't see the person. He deserved his suffering, after all.

And they hated Jesus when his healing touch restored the man born blind to community and family.

Both Mary and Martha grieved so deeply, but in their time women were not considered fully human. They saw Jesus as the one coming into the world to save the world, and Jesus saw them as the true witnesses they were. He shared their tears. They shared the joy of resurrection.

And, God loved him, Thomas, who was not ready to accept the testimony of others, at least when confronted with the evidence comes to utter those incredible words, "My Lord and my God!"

It takes us working together to help make the invisible visible, and to make God visible, through our faith in Jesus Christ, to the forgotten, the suffering, the abused, the reviled, and the depressed.

The more of us who work together, the more we see each other, and lift each other into visibility.

I started out by talking about something you can't see, but it's out there — dark matter. But there's something else out there in the great beyond we can't see either — a black hole. Not one of us has seen a black hole but we take their existence as a matter of faith.

A black hole, for those keeping score, is a massive star that collapses in on itself after burning up all its fuel. It's a frightening and awe-inspiring concept, because once it collapses its gravitational force is so great it can draw in planets, stars, and everything else, including light. That boundary at the edge of a black hole, called the Event Horizon, sucks in everything. You cannot see the black hole itself, which is called the Singularity. Even though everyone knows it's there from all the stuff that's disappearing inside, you can't see it.

There's a massive black hole at the center of our galaxy, but we can't see it. At least we couldn't, until just a couple years ago. In 2019, a team of scientists from around the world working together at their different telescopes, together created a worldwide telescope that actually photographed a black hole.

Harvard University's Shep Doeleman was a member of the team that took the photograph, and the director of what was called the Event Horizon Telescope Project. When working for funding he explained to Congress how it is important to reveal that which is hidden from our sight. As an example, he pointed to Robert Hooke, who published a drawing of a flea that he saw in a microscope, way back in 1655. He talked about how the first x-ray photos revealed what our bones looked like. Both events opened up a whole new world of knowledge.

"These are iconic images; they're terrifying, but we can't look away," he said. ...the invisible has become visible, and that maybe it's the beginning of something new, not just the end."

It's astounding that scientists from around the world could work as one to photograph something we can't see. Did you ever think what it would be like to have a church united across the planet that could not only seek the suffering that causes souls to sink into their own black hole of despair, but draws them out to be healed in the light of Jesus Christ? A world-wide church would not need to share the same administrative structure, the same policies, or worry about whether we're baptizing, breaking bread, and singing hymns exactly the same way. The church must be united in serving Jesus, in making the love of Jesus visible to a suffering world, and drawing all to our Lord so that at the name of Jesus every knee will bow.

The Word made flesh, the light of the world, came to take away the sin of the world, the condition of sin that keeps us apart. Let us resolve, like John the Baptist, to peel away the darkness and proclaim, "Behold the lamb of God! Behold the Word made flesh. Behold the light of the world." Reach out in Christ. Reach out in the name of Christ.

Amen.

Next!

Thanks to the movie, "American Underdog" the story of Kurt Warner is becoming familiar to a new generation of NFL fans who may know Warner solely as a talented football analyst. Warner aspired, like so many kids, to become an NFL quarterback, but after playing at Northern Iowa from 1990 to 1993, he was not drafted by any professional team. He got a tryout with the Green Bay Packers, but he was released before the 1994 season began.

Unlike professional baseball, where there are minor leagues for young players to develop their talents, most football players nowadays only have that one shot to make the pros. However, during the late '90s something called Arena Football was thriving. It was a claustrophobic sport, played indoors by six player teams on fields barely fifty yards long. It was mostly a passing game, showcasing quarterbacks and receivers, with lots of scoring and fans sitting close enough to touch the players.

Warner played three seasons with the Iowa Barnstormers of that Arena Football League. After that, he got a tryout in 1997 with the Bears which did not work out because of an injury to his throwing arm caused by a spider bite. However, he kept plugging away, working whatever job he could find, like stocking shelves in a grocery store, to make ends meet. Arena Football did not pay all the bills.

When the St. Louis Rams showed some interest, they sent him to NFL Europe, another short-lived minor league, where he played for the Amsterdam Admirals.

He did so well that he was signed to the Rams 1998 roster, but as the third string quarterback. He barely threw a pass all season. The situation was not much better as the 1999 season began, until an injury to the team's starting quarterback late in preseason meant that Warner would finally get his chance to start for an NFL team.

Improbably, but famously, Kurt Warner played so well he was voted the Most Valuable Player in the NFL. And it didn't stop there. He not only led the Rams to the Super Bowl Championship but was also named MVP of the game.

His career lasted twelve years, with two more Super Bowl appearances and another MVP award. He became famous as the quarterback who was stocking shelves at a grocery store when his big chance came, and he would use his unlikely story as a platform for sharing his deep Christian faith, which developed over time through the many hard knocks he experienced.

Now it seems obvious he was destined for glory but that's only in retrospect. There was every opportunity for discouragement and failure. Yet, in a way, it's a fairly typical story in the National Football League, where they talk about the philosophy of "next man up." Many players exist on the margins of the NFL, playing on practice squads. They used to call them taxi squads because these players had to have a job on the side, like driving a taxi, to make up for the small amount they are paid to suit up for practice and play against the regulars.

But sooner or later there's an injury, and when that happens, whoever's next needs to be ready to step up, with no excuses, to play. You may end up playing a totally unfamiliar position, or in a system you never learned, but no one cares about that. You have to play. No excuses.

And who knows? You might just become the next Kurt Warner.

In today's passage from the Gospel of Matthew, I think the evangelist is telling us that to some extent that the starting prophet has gone down with an injury, and Jesus is the understudy who's been waiting his chance and is now going to be a star.

And not just a star, but the most valuable player on the championship team.

Part of the problem with our perspective is that we're so used to thinking of John the Baptist as second string. He is always pictured as subservient to Jesus. He said himself he was not worthy to loose the sandal of the one who would follow him.

But John the Baptist was a big deal. The Jewish historian Josephus certainly thought so. After a military defeat by Herod Antipas, a son of Herod the Great who reigned over a portion of the kingdom of his father, Josephus wrote:

Now, some of the Jews thought that the destruction of Herod's army came from God, and that very justly, as a punishment of what he did against John, that was called the Baptist; for Herod slew him, who was a good man…. Herod…feared lest the great influence John had over the people might put it into his power and inclination to raise a rebellion (for they seemed ready to do anything he should advise,) thought it best, by putting him to death, to prevent any mischief he might cause…." (*Antiquities of the Jews*, book 18, chapter 5, section 2).

John the Baptist was a threat, simply because people listened to him, and he was fearless. He was not afraid to tell the secret of Herod Antipas, who stole his second wife Herodias from his brother Philip. Herodias willingly consented to the theft, as she was politically ambitious and thought she would go farther married to the other brother.

This was the second time Herodias was married to someone who was also her uncle. This was forbidden by the law of Moses, but most of the religious authorities had no intention of calling out Herod for this. Arguing with Herod could have been fatal.

John the Baptist had no trouble speaking truth to power, and that was one good reason for his arrest. Eventually, because of a drunken promise made by Herod to Herodias' daughter, John would be executed. However, while in prison he remained powerful and influential. Considering that Herod was worried that Jesus was not so much Jesus, as he was John the Baptist back from the dead (Matthew 14:2), it's clear that the Baptist left a large footprint.

Anyway, Matthew makes it clear that with the arrest of John Jesus is now in the lineup for Galilee, which may not be Jerusalem and the major leagues, but it was a starting assignment. As Matthew said, "From that time Jesus began to proclaim, "Repent, for the kingdom of heaven has come near" (4:17).

We think of Jesus as the obvious Son of God, but Jesus had

a lot of obstacles to overcome before playing in the big leagues. First of all, he suffered from the "wasn't born here" syndrome. Jesus was born in Bethlehem, which wasn't Jerusalem, and then became a refugee in Egypt around the age of two. He would have been living in the Jewish community of some Egyptian city, but the other kids would have reminded him he "talked funny."

Then, after the death of Herod the Great, the family did not return to Bethlehem, where he was born but instead moved to Nazareth, Mary's hometown. The only reason that Joseph, a Bethlehem boy, didn't move back where Jesus was born was because he was warned about Herod Antipas in a dream.

Because of the miraculous nature of Mary's pregnancy, there would still have been people who thought the worst of her and her son, and so Jesus would still grow up an outsider, never quite fully accepted. And if the people of Nazareth never quite accepted Jesus (and he was later rejected there), Nazareth itself was no place to come from, even if the attribution was a mistake. What did Nathaniel say about Jesus when he was first told about him, in an effort to get a cheap throwaway laugh? "Can anything good come out of Nazareth?" (1:46).

Actually, when Jesus was called to be the starter, I wouldn't have blamed him if he decided to keep his head down until there was a change in the political climate. What could it hurt?

Instead, he threw the gauntlet down, directly at Herod Antipas and the rest of the Herods, quoting Isaiah 9:2 when he said:
"Land of Zebulun, land of Naphtali, on the road by the sea, across the Jordan, Galilee of the Gentiles — the people who sat in darkness have seen a great light, and for those who sat in the region and shadow of death light has dawned" (Matthew 4:15-16). Who are the people who walked in darkness? Isaiah was originally challenging King Ahaz, who refused to trust in God and God's prophet, and instead threw in his lot with the Assyrian king Tiglath-pileser, because he thought it was politically safer. He thought this would prevent a confederation of two kings from overthrowing him, but Isaiah knew the Assyrians were the greater danger.

Isaiah was saying that the next king up was already born,

and he would be the light to the people who walk in darkness.

Matthew used the images from that passage, especially the light in the darkness, to demonstrate that the Herod dynasty, politically aligned with another nation-swallowing empire, that of the Romans, was toast. The new king, King Jesus, had arrived.

Jesus then called his first disciples, Simon and Andrew. Unlike the Herods, who are suspicious that others will supplant them, Jesus fearlessly calls people who will replace him after he is gone. In the sentence "I will make you fish for people..." the verb translated as "make" really means, in this context, "I will equip you." Jesus intended to train his replacements, to make them disciples, not just converts.

Jesus commanded them to follow him and without knowing what that meant, they did. Over the next several chapters they watched Jesus, grew with Jesus, and heard his words — especially the Sermon on the Mount which will soon follow, before Jesus asked them, "Who do people say that I am?" And by that time, they knew the answer. They may not fully understand it. The gospels made it clear that not until after the cross did the disciples fully understand what it meant to be a follower of Jesus, but it's a start.

Remember, we are never fully equipped. We're never fully ready, when our turn comes to jump into the starting lineup. I like to point to the resurrection appearance of Jesus to his apostles in Galilee, where the eleven apostles stood before their risen Lord, and even there Matthew said, "...but some doubted... (28:17)." Even now, when we are called into the breach, ready to take part in the Great Commission:

"Go therefore and make disciples of all nations, baptizing them in the name of the Father and of the Son and of the Holy Spirit, and teaching them to obey everything that I have commanded you (28:19-20)."

We may not feel fully ready, but we're in the game!

This generation of apostles and disciples would be arrested and martyred for their witness. But others would take their place in the starting lineup. They too would become MVPs and champions of the faith.

Now it's our turn.

When you're thrown into the lineup, don't make excuses. Be ready. We may not be called to be martyrs. We may become missionaries. But board chairs, quilters, Sunday school teachers, cookie bakers, and cleaner-after-uppers, all of us step into someone else's shoes, and carry on, and pass the torch, or the broom when it is time.

Just as Jesus promised his first disciples, he equipped them to become fishers for Christ, so we, through the experiences we have gained over time, will become the one who types up the bulletin, goes to youth events, volunteers to pull weeds, and mops the floors. We'll become the ones who dry wall at disaster sites or take training so we can work disaster relief child care.

Don't just prepare to be the next one up. Expect it. Assume it.

Don't be afraid, if you've been doing one sort of ministry for a long time, to pass it along to someone else, without waiting to be injured, so you can assume another ministry where someone is needed, and you've got this feeling that someone is you.

Maybe Jesus would have rather played for Green Bay — I mean Jerusalem, originally, but that prophecy from Isaiah made it clear that great things could happen in St. Louis, ah, Galilee of the Gentiles. What matters is that through our efforts "The people who sat in darkness have seen a great light, and for those who sat in the region and shadow of death, light has dawned."

The ministry of Jesus is described as one of proclaiming the good news and bringing healing to a struggling community. Out of our struggles, our seeming failures, our disappointments, and most of all, our persistence in obedience to the example of Jesus through all of it, our refusal to quit as disciples in the face of setbacks, we are preparing to proclaim the good news of the kingdom, to bring healing to a suffering world, and to become, at a time of God's choosing, to be the MVP we are destined to be.

Amen.

Fourth Sunday after the Epiphany
Matthew 5:1-12

Tables Turned

Jokes fall into different categories: Shaggy Dog, Put-Downs, Paradox, Wordplay, but in the end they all involve something called Tables Turned. You think the joke is going in one direction, but suddenly there's a radical alteration in the point of view.

One of the simplest examples involves two cavemen. One hollers out, "Hurry! A saber-toothed tiger is attacking your mother-in-law." To which the first caveman replies, "What do I care what happens to some saber-toothed tiger?"

Now I don't know how many laughs Jesus got when he delivered the series of one-liners we call the Beatitudes, the opening salvos of what we call the Sermon on the Mount, but I'll bet there were chuckles, some rueful, as well as plenty of smiles when Jesus spoke to the people about a world where the tables are turned in favor of those who mourn, the poor in spirit, the peacemakers, the meek, the merciful, the pure in heart, and all those who are persecuted for righteousness's sake.

Because the rich and the powerful don't like being the butt of a joke, I'm sure there were some who stomped off.

You know, Jesus was a funny guy. He told parables set in the real world, where things are turned inside out and there are surprising endings. Think about that woman turning her house inside out looking for that coin. Or the parables we *should* call "the shocking Samaritan" or "the faithful but bitter brother." We've been there.

The Beatitudes are game changers. They are shockers and they are for all of us.

They are worth the effort. Jesus walked up the mountain and others thought it was worthwhile to follow. It can be work to unpack these words of wisdom, but I think it's worth the effort.

Not everyone has agreed through the ages. The Sermon on the Mount in general, and the Beatitudes in particular, call for a shocking change of attitude about the world because the tables are about to be turned. Turning the other cheek, loving your enemies, doing good for those who hate you — powerful people don't like to hear these kinds of things. During much of Christian history good biblical literalists have done their best to explain away these commands of Jesus by something they called the two kingdom theory.

Basically this excuse boils down to this: Jesus delivered this sermon to his disciples. That's what it says at the start of this passage: "When Jesus saw the crowds, he went up the mountain; and after he sat down, his disciples came to him" (5:1). Therefore, the theory goes, whatever Jesus said in the Sermon on the Mount is only for people like the apostles — monks, nuns, hermits, those who had a special calling. The rest of us should go on hating our enemies, taking revenge on those who wronged us, and looking on with lust at others. Kings can still lay waste to kingdoms, hold their own people in subjection, and otherwise occupy themselves with the things kings do, and still be assured of salvation.

At the start of the sermon, Jesus specifically invited his disciples to climb up the mountain with him to hear his words, but when the sermon ends its clear everybody seeking him must have followed them, for the Sermon on the Mount concluded, "Now when Jesus had finished saying these things, the crowds were astounded at his teaching…." (7:28). The implication is clear. The crowds also followed the disciples to hear what Jesus had to say.

They followed to hear what he had to say began with this series of *blesseds*. The term "blessed" is a translation of the Greek word *"makairos."* It is sometimes translated "happy," and refers to the deep, spiritual joy that paradoxically is given to those who live godly lives.

Sayings beginning with *blessed* are not unique to Jesus. In pagan literature those who were blessed lived in the same state of mind as the gods. In the Psalms the blessed were aligned with

God's principles for living a "godly" life. Blesseds were not only to hear, but to do!

Still, these nine blesseds stood out because of their sheer number. This was not an isolated comment. The Beatitudes built on each other.

What did Jesus mean in the first Beatitude: "Blessed are the poor in spirit, for theirs is the kingdom of heaven"? Some have suggested these are not the economically poor, but in the ancient world, and in the New Testament, this particular word always refers to the poor.

In the Roman Empire, almost everybody was poor. Some lived hand to mouth, and many more were slaves. Only a few were rich. One of the Jewish denominations of the time, the Sadducees, many of whom were rich and powerful, did not believe in an afterlife, so they believed that wealth was a sign God favored you. Poverty was a state people deserved because God did not like you. The poor and rich were being punished and rewarded in this life with what they deserved.

The phrase *poor in spirit*, which is found nowhere else in the New Testament, referred most likely to the emotional and spiritual state of the forsaken poor. Poverty is not sought. It is not a goal. Historically, it's how most people lived.

In the first sermon Jesus proclaimed, recorded in the gospel of Luke, our Savior opened the Isaiah scroll and began to read, "The spirit of the Lord God is upon me, because the Lord has anointed me; he has sent me to bring good news to the oppressed…"(Isaiah 61:1). As we will see, these words of the prophet made it clear God's anointed would proclaim a Jubilee year, when debts were forgiven, land was restored, and hope was granted unto the poor. This first bold statement had to anger the rich and powerful. If the poor in spirit lived a humble life, they were to recognize that this was not forever. God's blessings would be rich and eternal.

Blessed are those who mourn, for they will be comforted. Grief because of loss was also a universal condition. Sorrow was a journey with no landmarks. Simply saying our loved ones are in a better place does not relieve the bitter place we inhabit. Here

Jesus again stated that our ultimate destiny is one of comfort and release from the pain of mourning, restating what he said in his first sermon that he had come, as Isaiah prophesized, "…to comfort all who mourn… to give them a garland instead of ashes, the oil of gladness instead of mourning (Isaiah 61:2-3)." Through all the stages of grief, Jesus is walking with us, however long that journey takes.

Psalm 37:11 is at the heart of the next Beatitude. The psalmist knew how hard it was to live meekly in a world where violence and intimidation reign, but after noting "Yet a little while, and the wicked will be no more," he stated: "*But the meek shall inherit the land, and delight themselves in abundant prosperity.*" That's exactly what Jesus said: "Blessed are the meek, for they will inherit the earth." The difference here is that neither poverty nor mourning was a desired state, either in the ancient world or now. They were just depressingly common. Meekness, however, was recognized as a desirable trait in ancient times, and something to be cultivated. Yet then, as now, all of us know it is hard to achieve. Here Jesus was encouraging us to achieve a state of mind, instead of transcending it.

Blessed are those who hunger and thirst for righteousness, for they will be filled. While the first Beatitude spoke of the literally poor, and both hunger and thirst are as deplorable as poverty, here Jesus was talking about a specific desire — for justice! The fact that so many of us like to read mysteries and police procedurals, plu watch movies and television shows with solving a crime and balancing the books — think of shows like "The Equalizer" — it's clear we'd like to see all the loose ends tied up in a nice bow. We want to see the guilty punished, the innocent released, and those who have been harmed to experience some measure of restoration. Because the world is complicated that doesn't always happen. But Jesus assured us, in God's time, it will.

Blessed are the merciful, for they shall receive mercy. Mercy is part of God's nature — "The Lord is merciful and gracious, slow to anger, and abounding in steadfast love and faithfulness…"(Exodus 34:6). As it says in this beatitude in Proverbs: "…he that hath mercy on the poor, happy is he." (Proverbs 14:21 KJV) This one is mathematical. You want mercy? Be merciful.

In Psalm 24 the question was asked, "Who shall ascend the hill of the Lord?" The answer: "Those who have clean hands and pure hearts..." (Psalm 24:4). While to some extent it is presumed we'll know what Jesus meant by the pure in heart when he said *"Blessed are the pure in heart, for they will see God,"* the term itself suggests that becoming pure in heart requires us to do some scrubbing. It is a rare thing to "see God" in Hebrew scriptures. We're told at the end of Deuteronomy that Moses "knew God face to face" (Deuteronomy 34:10) in a way like no other, yet in Exodus 24:9-11 Moses and over seventy other elders saw God.

Things got controversial when Jesus said, "Blessed are the peacemakers, for they shall be called the children of God." We're okay if people live peacefully, but not okay with Jesus telling us not to wage war. And this is an interesting word — peace *making*. One is not to stand on the sideline, but to actively work for peace. The Hebrew word behind it all, *shalom,* is referring not just to a temporary cessation of hostilities required to arm up for the next war, but wholeness, wellness (not necessarily health), with God and with all people. We are blessed if we work for this, actively, seeking to mediate, to constructively improve lives so war is not necessary, to stand up against unjust military actions, and to call out leaders and call on believers to work for peace. I don't know what we can do to eliminate wars — but if we do nothing I'm not sure we can call ourselves children of God.

Christians have realized in all eras that if we're going to insist Jesus meant what he said and that we are meant to live like him, we will be persecuted — yet blessed. *Blessed are those who are persecuted for righteousness' sake, for theirs is the kingdom of heaven.*

We are talking of a kingdom that exists both in heaven, where we will be rewarded, but also a reign of God upon the earth, where sometimes we see little sign that Jesus is recognized as Lord. But as John the Revelator wrote: "Here is a call for the endurance of the saints, those who keep the commandments of God and hold fast to the faith of Jesus" (Revelation 14:12).

That leads us to the last Beatitude, which not only expands on this one, but deliberately changes from the third-person plural to the second-person plural — "y'all."

Blessed are you when people revile you and persecute you and utter all kinds of evil against you falsely on my account. Rejoice and be glad, for your reward is great in heaven, for in the same way they persecuted the prophets who were before you.

It's "y'all" which is us, and "my account," which is Jesus saying "me." You and me. We are in this together, and for this reason the tables are turned dramatically. We are seen to suffer, and we do suffer, but the result will be rejoicing and gladness, now and in heaven.

Jesus was putting us in the picture, both in the scriptural account and the heavenly picture, and we see this most clearly in Revelation — where Satan, having been cast to earth following an unsuccessful rebellion against heaven, set up the beast who corrupted the people and intensified the persecution of those who stood fast with Jesus. Yet very quickly the angels proclaimed the victory of the Lord, the judgment of God against the forces of darkness, and the vindication of the blessed! (See Revelation 12-14).

And this is followed by another Beatitude, another blessed: *And I heard a voice from heaven saying, "Write this: Blessed are the dead who from now on die in the Lord." "Yes," says the Spirit, "they will rest from their labors, for their deeds follow them."* (Revelation 14;13).

Blessed indeed.

Just a few weeks ago, when preaching about the refugee Jesus, I had the chance to mention the Getty Museum in Los Angeles, where many paintings with biblical themes are preserved for all of us. One of the greatest works of art is also one of the smallest. You could walk right by "The Sermon on the Mount," by the Flemish artist Jan Brueghel the Elder (1568-1625). Painted in 1598, using oil based paints on copper, it measures 10 ½ by 14 ½ inches. But if you take just a glance you'll be caught in its snare.

Under a leafy landscape, high above a distant city, Jesus is speaking these words of life to over a hundred people. Jesus and his disciples seem to be dressed in what I would call biblical costumes, but everyone else is dressed in sixteenth-century Flemish fashions.

As I zoom in on the people, and then slowly pan across the painting, notice the detail given to every person in this painting. Some were listening with rapt attention to every word Jesus said. Some were distracted by what was going on nearby. People were coming and going, people with their own cares and problems. How about that man and the small child at the bottom of the painting. Were they begging? Would someone live the words of Jesus and share? All these people were hearing through their own filters. Some pointed to Jesus and commented on what he was saying. Did they agree? Were they being critical? Little groups gossip. Were they even talking about Jesus? Probably not. Someone was selling what looked like pretzels. Others were still approaching. They would only catch part of what was being said.

The miracle was that in the midst of all this chaos somebody heard. Somebody passed it along. And that is our job. Despite the cares of our lives, and the distractions, we are the evangelists. The thing is, we don't have to board a boat or catch a plane in order to spread the words of Jesus around the world. We can do it from our seat here in church, right in the middle of this sermon.

But pay attention for just a moment more before you go out into the world, please. I want to explain what I mean.

In Jesus' day as in most of human history these words of his were not read from a printed Bible, but heard and repeated. I don't know that anyone was taking notes at the time when Jesus first proclaimed the Beatitudes, but my guess is that those who heard compared what they remembered with each other. They spoke about these things, and what they meant for their lives. Who were the poor in spirit? What was the righteousness of God? What did it mean to be a peacemaker? It would be decades before Matthew wrote down these words, but people had been sharing them all that time.

That's us! In this digital age of social media, there is so much content out there that there might as well be no content. Not everyone out there is going to crack open their Bible. Indeed, most people out there are only going to hear these words because you post them on your Facebook page, or pass them along through your social media channels. You are now the channel for the word of God.

Heard — held to heart — repeated.

Amen.

Two More For The Nativity Set

If a movie's a hit you can count on a sequel.

Certainly you'll need some of the same characters because we want to know what happens next to them, but you've got to add a couple new ones that bring a whole new perspective, and the possibility of some added plot twists none of us ever thought of.

It's hard to beat the nativity of Jesus when it comes to a great story. There have been all kinds of filmed adaptations of the story. I mean, Mary, Joseph, the angels, some shepherds, and of course the baby Jesus. Since animals are great scene stealers, sheep, cows, and probably a dog or a cat thrown in make this a tough combination to top.

But what about Nativity II — The Sequel? This *time it's not just about the baby.*

I'm surprised no one's tried to make this film. After, it comes with two new characters — Simeon and Anna, who have two very different outlooks on what happened in the first movie. And we know that the ending of the first story — *and they lived happily ever after* — was never going to work anyway. If we go with Simeon and Anna for the sequel, that left Herod, the magi, and the flight into Egypt for Nativity III — *Run For Your Life!*

Let's stop and look at Simeon and Anna, shall we? Now one thing that Luke made clear is that the family of Jesus weren't rich, but they made sure to observe the religious obligations. So it's no surprise that eight days after his birth Joseph and Mary made the five mile trip from Bethlehem to Jerusalem, walked up the hill through the city to get to the temple, and presented Jesus as per custom. (By the way, if you're asking why didn't Mary ride the donkey, it's because I doubt very much if there was a donkey to ride on. That's part of the Christmas card Christmas, not the real world Christmas.)

A little sixties nostalgia. In the song "California Dreamin'" the Mamas and the Papas remember how they went into a church at one point in their pilgrimage, fell on their knees, and prayed. Some of us remember a time decades ago when churches were left open as a matter of course and people could go in to pray or reflect or just rest.

But Jesus lived in a time when the temple was open 24/7, which is why Simeon and Anna are both here to see the presentation of Jesus in the temple.

Jesus was presented at the temple to be circumcised, but also to be named. His name was Jesus — Yeshua — Joshua — God saves — God rescues — God delivers.

Leviticus 12:6-8 mandated the sacrifice of a sheep on the occasion of the presentation of a child. That could have been an expensive proposition, so the passage also provided a less expensive alternative. Joseph and Mary took advantage of this second option. When it came to Sunday school class parties, youth conventions, going out as a group, or working together to improve the church building, there needs to be sensitivity that people are not excluded, and this needs tact as well as the willingness on the part of some to give discretely, without recognition or acknowledgement. There needs to be ways in which people can give in kind rather than in quantity. There is nothing second rate or second class about the offering of these young parents in the temple.

Simeon and Anna were both named as prophets in this familiar passage about the presentation of Jesus in the temple. This is all we knew about those two, and it may well have been that this was the most significant moment in their lives. If so, it came in their later years. Then again, maybe there were greater things they accomplished, but we simply don't know what from the scripture record. What we do know is you could find them in the house of worship if you needed them. Their commitment to faith and practice was lifelong. I'm not sure if any of us can say we've experienced the most significant moment in our lives, but what we do know is we'd better keep our eyes and our hearts open, because the Holy Spirit is active and present at all moments.

Luke told us that the prophet Anna never left the temple, but worshiped there with fasting and prayer night and day. Anna was ancient by everyone's standards, and especially in a time when the average life span was 25 to thirty years.

The Greek can be interpreted two ways. It may mean Anna was 84-years-old when she found Jesus in the temple. However Luke may be inviting us to add Anna's age when she married — perhaps fourteen, say — to the seven years of her marriage and her 94 years of widowhood. The total is more like 105. She was ancient indeed. Though she was labeled a prophetess, a title given to Miriam sister of Moses, Deborah, Huldah, and the wife of Isaiah, she was silent at first. Why? We don't always need a running commentary on what was going on. Sometimes we can see for ourselves. There doesn't have to be an Instagram report. It's not always necessary to tweet. We don't need a text or an email. In the face of true glory, and our salvation, and the babe who would be king, Anna said nothing. We can do worse.

We are told Anna was the daughter of Phanuel, which is the Greek version of Peniel — that is what Jacob named the place where he wrestled a mysterious figure all night long. Peniel means "face of God." That's appropriate, because when Anna finally spoke, it was to let others know that she had seen the face of God!

This was also when Mary met Simeon. Simeon's name comes from the Hebrew word Shema, the word for *hear - listen*! That was at the heart of the Shema, the prayer from Deuteronomy 6:4-5, which is prayed at every synagogue service — "Hear, O Israel: the Lord is our God, the Lord is alone. You shall love the Lord your God with all your heart, and with all your soul, and with all your might."

Simeon began with a statement that was peaceful, joyful, yet melancholy: "Master, now you are dismissing your servant in peace, according to your word; for my eyes have seen your salvation...." (Luke 2:29). The older we get, the more we can't help but reflect on the wonders new babies will experience long after we are gone.

There's some of that melancholy, too, in the words of the Rev.

Dr. Martin Luther King Jr., who, on the night before he died, told a crowd in Memphis, Tennessee, "We've got some difficult days ahead. But it really doesn't matter with me now, because I've been to the mountaintop...I've seen the promised land. I may not get there with you. But I want you to know tonight, that we, as a people, will get to the promised land."

These words of Simeon were a reminder that we're part of God's story, not the other way around. We have our turn on the stage, but it's not all about us. Others were here before us. Others will follow. And if we're grateful for anything, it's that we had a part to play, great or small.

The other thing Simeon did was tell the truth. "This child is destined for the falling and rising of man in Israel, and to be a sign that will be opposed so that the inner thoughts of many will be revealed—and a sword will pierce your own heart as well" (Luke 2:34).

This child will break your heart. You will see things and you won't be able to help. In the fourteenth century a devotional based on the concept of Mary's suffering became a focus for other Christians to meditate on their sorrows as well. In some traditions Mary is called "Our Lady of Sorrows," because of the seven sorrows she willingly endured. We find these all in scripture. These words of Simeon's were the first sorrow. Words of truth spoken soon after a child's birth may well be necessary to steel our hearts for the journey ahead. Any child can have an ailment, a condition, an ability, that will make the years ahead a challenge, but, Lord willing, ultimately a joy.

Life goes on. Kids grow up. Life is touched by sorrow, but ultimately joy as well. In the fourteenth century a devotional based on the concept of Mary's suffering became a focus for other Christians to meditate on their sorrows as well. Mary's sorrows included this prophecy of Samuel, with its warning that Mary's own heart would be pierced as the fortunes of many rose and fell.

Other sorrows would include the flight into Egypt, the time Mary and Joseph had no idea where Jesus was in Jerusalem, the occasion decades later when he publicly carried his cross, when he was crucified for all to see, when his body was taken down, and when he was laid in the tomb.

That's part of our pain as parents. More important — that's part of God's pain in giving us free will. Mary would not stop loving this baby when he left home and his responsibilities as the head of the household to do something greater, nor would she be able to save him from the cross, nor help to alleviate his sufferings.

Mary said yes to all these. So do we.

I began this message talking about sequels and the reason we have sequels is that we know deep down inside that nobody lives happily ever after. Real life intrudes. Perhaps you've seen the Stephen Sondheim musical *Into the Woods*. In Act 1 we meet many of our favorite fairy tale characters — Cinderella, Rapunzel, Jack of the beanstalk fame, Little Red Riding Hood, and more. Their lives are intertwined throughout Act 1 as they meet seemingly insurmountable challenges, but in the end all is well, and it's clear they're going to live — ah — happily ever after.

When the curtain goes up on Act 2 real life begins. The Prince abandons Cinderella, the baker is widowed, leaving him a single parent, and the giant's mother comes down from the clouds looking for Jack. The survivors struggle together, all scarred in one way or another, comforted by each other, and determined to tell their story.

Mary was one of the survivors, and her story became one of triumph. Jesus was raised. Later Mary was present with 120 others in the Upper Room when God's Spirit descended in their midst, joy filled her life — but as all of us who have survived great sorrows know, that doesn't take away the fact that sorrows are sorrows. We are still wounded — but our wounds are part of a tapestry that together present a whole life praising God and working for God's glory and the good of our neighbors.

Obeying the will of God does not free us from sorrows, nor does it insulate us from the consequences of all that life rains upon us, but our perspective has to be that of a rock climber, pausing to look down from a great height, their hands and knees scarred and bleeding from the scrapes and cuts that come from contact with the sharp edges of a sheer surface. We're amazed we've come so far, but we're aware we have farther to go, and that the goal is glorious.

It sounds like there's a lot more to *Nativity 2 — The Sequel*, and that Mary's character gains a lot more depth thanks to the plot twists introduced by Simeon and Anna. It's going to be a glorious story.

Not only that, our story will be a glorious one as well. When Jesus was presented in the temple, Anna let everyone know this baby was the greatest thing that ever happened, and that's true for each one of us. We may not be the Messiah, but we're God's great gift to the world. And Simeon's words remind us that there will be many times of rising and falling and rising again in our lives and because of our lives. However, let's not forget what else Simeon said. He praised God, saying his time of departure, now come, was made more blessed by this moment of presence, in the present, where the presence of the Lord and Savior became reality.

And today, in the present, our presence, all of us bearing the marks of Christ's cross, but also lifted by the spirit of God's glory in both the death and the resurrection of Jesus, we may all, from this service, depart in peace. Be a light for the revealing of this glory to the nations, and for the glory to God's people, here in this place, and wherever the rising and falling of life takes us.

Amen.

Salt And Light

Rufus P. Bucher (1883-1956) was an Old Order Dunker minister, an evangelist, and farmer. He lived in a small town called Unicorn. For 55 years he served in the free ministry as an elder and the pastor of the Mechanic Grove, Pennsylvania, congregation.

In addition, he was the presiding elder of six other congregations, moderator of district meeting ten times, and the Annual Conference in 1946. He served on the district mission board for forty years. The extent of his evangelistic work was impressive — more than 200 series of meetings around the country.

He was also a writer, authoring several books about the gospel, living it, as well as believing in it.

One day Bucher was returning by train from a revival meeting when he was handed a tract titled "Brother, Are You Saved?" by an earnest young man who must have thought there was something about his fellow passenger that marked him as a lost soul. After a pause the young man asked the big question: "Are you saved?"

Bucher paused, then said, "That is a good question and deserves an answer. I think, however, that I might be prejudiced in my own behalf. You'd better go down to Quarryville and ask George Hensel, the hardware merchant, what he thinks about it. Or you might go to the Mechanic Grove grocer or to one of my neighbors in Unicorn. While there you might ask my wife and children. I'll be ready to let their answers stand as my own."

No doubt there was a twinkle in his eye when Bucher retold that story, but his point was that simply saying you were saved was no proof that you are. People will say anything to get rid of somebody in sales — especially when their product is Jesus.

No, you might *say* anything, but it's what you *do* that speaks volumes. This is why Jesus said, in today's passage, "…let your light shine before others, so that they may see your good works and give glory to your Father in heaven" (Matthew 5:16). Having shared the extraordinary beatitudes that were the foundation of the Sermon on the Mount, Jesus addressed all those who were listening to demonstrate what it meant to be meek, merciful, and pure in heart.

It meant, among other things, listening to the word of God. The words of God are salt and light.

And so are we.

If you've seen the stage play "Godspell," (not the movie — this song doesn't appear in it), there are great lyrics written by Stephen Schwartz called "Learn Your Lessons Well." It outlined how important it is for people to listen and learn the good book, using that as a foundation so you can live the commandments. As it says, first to read the words, then heed the words because one never knows when one will need the words….look the lyrics up online (they are under copyright).

In the same way we're called to ingest God's word and become ourselves salt and light.

In our time, the salt shaker on the table is a common sight. Salt is inexpensive. It's everywhere. The supply seems inexhaustible. Anyone driving on Interstate 80 across the salt flats between Salt Lake City, Utah, and Wendover, Nevada, can't help but be impressed by miles of salt, and the huge mounds — nay, mountains — harvested by salt companies, waiting to be transported.

Indeed, if the salt shaker is missing, it's not because we can't afford it, but because our doctor has asked us to eliminate it due to its contributing to high blood pressure and heart disease.

And as anyone who's been asked to no longer consume salt, there is no real substitute for it. All the salt substitutes remind us that we're craving real salt!

But the pervasive presence of salt is a modern situation. Throughout the ages salt has been rare, hard to find and tough, even dangerous, to mine, a form of currency, a reason for trade,

124

and most of all, essential for life. The problem has been how to get enough salt to stay alive and remain healthy!

There's the famous phrase "below the salt," used for those who did not rank high enough to sit at the end of the table where the salt was placed. Roman soldiers were sometimes paid in salt because they could spend that anywhere in the Empire.

Salt is a mark of friendship. In Kazakhstan, you greet visitors by giving them bread and salt. Since Russian space travelers, and all others from whatever country they come from who travel with them, land in Kazakhstan, they are always greeted with these traditional elements when they return to earth.

In the Wisdom of Sirach, one of the books included in the Apocrypha, the wise sage says,

> *The basic necessities of human life*
> *are water and fire and iron and salt*
> *and wheat flour and milk and honey,*
> *the blood of the grape and oil and clothing* (Sirach 39:26).

When Ezra wished to inform King Artaxerxes that political intrigue by his opponents had slowed the rebuilding of the temple to a halt, he wrote, " *Now because we share the salt of the palace and it is not fitting for us to witness the king's dishonor, therefore we send and inform the king...* (Ezra 4:14).

When King of Abijah of Judah was about to give battle to King Jeroboam of Israel he attempted one last negotiation by reminding him "*...the Lord God of Israel gave the kingship over Israel forever to David and his sons by a covenant of salt?*" (2 Chronicles 13:5).

And the Apostle Paul, addressing the Colossians, reminded them how important it was to choose their words carefully, in order to create a good impression for all Christians: " *Conduct yourselves wisely toward outsiders, making the most of the time. Let your speech always be gracious, seasoned with salt, so that you may know how you ought to answer everyone* (Colossians 4:5).

There's nothing more useful than salt. Loyalty, friendship, life itself, all depend on salt.

So when Jesus told us, "You are the salt of the earth…" he was telling us we were and are valuable, that we are essential to life, that others crave the salt of the good news of Jesus Christ, and that our presence in the world is vital, and indeed, craved. We're not just a few grains of salt in a throwaway paper shaker from a fast food restaurant. We matter!

Now what did Jesus mean when he added "…*but if salt has lost its taste, how can its saltiness be restored? It is no longer good for anything, but is thrown out and trampled under foot.*"

Chemically, salt will be salt. But if you mix it up with things that are impure — if you mix it with mud, for instance, it's just gunk. It's useless. Keep your focus on who we are — we are those who are living kingdom life. We turn the other cheek. We love our enemies. We are the peacemakers, the merciful, the pure of heart. We are salt. We improve everyone's life. We're essential for life.

Jesus continued, *"You are the light of the world."* Like salt, light is foundational. In Genesis, even before there's the sun, moon, and stars, God created light. It is the first act of creating order. There's the primeval chaos, the world that was, the abyss, chaos, the waters, but the Spirit of God hovered over the waters, chaos was repelled, and God said, "Let there be light." The universe was changed! Now God's story could begin.

This is reiterated in the Gospel of John, where we are told that the word is life, and "…the life was the light of all people. The light shined in the darkness, and the darkness did not overcome it." A little further on John got even more specific, talking how Jesus is "The true light, which enlightens everyone…" (John 1:4-5,9).

To understand just how we are the ones who cast that light with others, and what a change it makes, consider this verse from Proverbs: *Those who are generous are blessed, for they share their bread with the poor* (Proverbs 22:9).

This involved a little bad science but good theology. The ancients believed that the eye sent forth light which illuminated the things we see. In other words, the eye was the source of light.

Light shot from your eye and bounced off objects, coming back to you. So what you see and how you see it makes a difference — between evil wishes or hope.

They believed in the evil eye — looking at someone with malice could harm them. And that's true, regardless of the science. We've all heard the saying, "If looks could kill...." In a certain sense they do. This proverb emphasized the opposite. Instead of the evil eye, it speaks of the good eye. The words for good eye are translated as "generous" in most translations. Those who look on the poor with the good eye bless both themselves and those who they help.

We can look with the good eye at the marginalized, the suffering, and the struggling. Keeping in line with the Sermon on the Mount, our eye can be on those who mourn, providing comfort, on the meek, helping them inherit the earth, on the peacemakers, so that all who see them in our light will know they are children of God.

Our light, shooting out of our eyes — again, I know that's not how light works, and Jesus no doubt knew this too, but Jesus was speaking in terms people understood then and this is what Jesus is telling us now — makes us the city on the hill. We want to be seen. We don't want to hide our lamp under a bushel basket where we can no longer help people. We shine our light and people see good works and give the glory to our Father in heaven.

Let's take a look at the painting we talked about last week — "The Sermon on the Mount," by Jan Brueghel the Elder. We see Jesus, preaching the sermon that guided Christian living. He was the source of the light.

Slide all the way down to the bottom of the painting, and go a little to the left. There is a small circle of people. A barefoot man in red, blue, and white, looking not a bit well, has his hands out, begging for help. Notice the attention the painter gave to painting him barefoot when so many around him are wearing shoes. To his right is a barefoot child, arms raised in a gesture crying for help. Proceeding further to the right, there is a woman holding another child who is eating something, and a man, seated, his head bound in bandages, seeming to smile with gratitude. The man they were looking toward had taken the hand of the one begging for help. He was giving them all his attention. The child who was eating something, perhaps the man with the good eye bought him one of the pretzels being sold just a bit to our right.

I don't know if the man with the good eye had heard much of what Jesus had to say, but he was living the Sermon on the Mount. What he was doing was happening in plain sight. Look at the attention he drew. One man, to his right, had turned away from the conversation that he was engaged in, and how *his* full attention was being given to the tableau. He was smiling in approval. Someone was hopefully learning a Bible lesson, bringing it to life.

What is emphasized throughout the Sermon on the Mount was not theoretical ethics drawn out of thin air. Jesus was drawing from the Torah, a word used sometimes to denote the first five books of the Bible but also means "The Way." Don't forget that according to the Acts of the Apostles, before believers in Antioch coined the term Christians, Christians referred to their faith as "The Way," which is another way of saying Torah.

Jesus was not teaching a new way. He was teaching *the* way, drawn from the holy scriptures. "Do not think I have come to abolish the law or the prophets," he said. "I have not come to abolish but to fulfill." Not one jot or tittle will be taken out of the law until it is fulfilled. Jot or tittle, literally one "iota" or "keraia," in the Greek. The iota refers to the smallest letter, the letter i which is the tiniest stroke of the pen. It is not dotted in Greek. The keraia, a word signifying 'horn,' is also a tiny stroke of the pen, and refers to the tiniest part of the Hebrew alphabet, where a small stroke can change what letter you're reading, and therefore the meaning.

Sometimes people ask, "Do we need the Old Testament?" as if it were obsolete, or superseded. They seem to imagine that there's this fierce, angry god in the Old Testament, and a kindly, gentle Jesus in the New Testament. Jesus is telling us nothing of the sort. It's like the author John Goldingay says in his book, deliberately titled *Why do we need the New Testament?*, that certainly we need the New Testament, but the gentle, loving God is in the old, while at the same time Jesus said some of the most challenging, difficult things. In other words, the things we like best in the New Testament are found in even greater abundance in the Hebrew scriptures. The kingdom of God is proclaimed even louder and more clearly by the prophets of old.

The key is interpretation. We are to interpret the way through Jesus, looking with the good eye of Jesus so that we can enlighten the world! In his day there were many different denominations of believers who interpreted the same scriptures differently. We sometimes think it was all the Pharisees, and they were all legalists, when nothing could have been further from the truth. Pharisees cared for the ordinary people, and provided the leadership in neighborhood synagogues. While we see a few of the worst Pharisees on display in the New Testament, many of them probably took delight in the way Jesus interpreted the scriptures.

In the next few Sundays we're going to learn more about what the law means when it comes to so many things but for now, think of this:

When you look at others, people you know and love, people you dislike, and total strangers, do you look with the love of Jesus, projecting the good eye, and in that light do others see Jesus? And are you the salt of the earth, valuable and blessed for who you are, made able to do God's good work in this world?

Amen.

(Need more stories about salt? See *Salt: A World History* by Mark Kurlansky, Walker and Company, 2002.)

Two Ways? Three Ways? One Way? Or, The Right Way?

My suspicion is that many of us learned, memorized, or at least studied a famous poem by the American poet Robert Frost (1874-1963) often called "The Road Less Traveled," that was originally titled simply "Two Roads." Do you remember it?

It begins simply "Two roads diverged in a yellow wood…" The poet describes a temporary indecision about which road he should take. He realized he couldn't walk down both, but eventually the poet makes a decision. The poem ends:

> I shall be telling this with a sigh
> Somewhere ages and ages hence:
> Two roads diverged in a wood, and I —
> I took the one less traveled by,
> And that has made all the difference.

What many of us don't know is that Frost wrote the poem for a friend who was struggling to make a momentous choice, and in his mind Frost thought the poem gently mocked indecision, suggesting that sometimes we overthink things, and the choice might not be as important as we thought.

His friend, however, understood the poem to mean if we made the wrong choice he might regret it bitterly in later years. It spurred his friend to make a quick choice — that cost him his life!

Frost's friend was the Englishman Edward Thomas (1878-1917), a successful writer who nevertheless thought of himself as a literary hack. Frost, who when they met in 1913 was largely unknown, had come to England hoping to jumpstart his writing career. The two met and become close companions.

The first World War broke out in 1914. Ultimately at least twenty million would die, and although at first it was considered by people on both sides as a sacred crusade, it has since come to be seen as a senseless conflict that both sides fell into almost by accident. Thomas was too old be conscripted, but he agonized over whether it was his duty to enlist anyway. Out of that turmoil he wrote a good deal of poetry that would ultimately be published posthumously and establish him in that era as a literary giant.

When Thomas received Frost's poem in 1915 he interpreted it to mean he had no choice but to enlist immediately, which he did. After training, during which he rose to the rank of second lieutenant, he was sent to the front. He died weeks later.

Sometimes it seems as if there are only two choices. Sometimes it seems as if every choice is so important we agonize over it as if it were a life or death matter.

Moses, in his farewell address to the people on the edge of the promised land, said, "See, I have set before you today life and prosperity, death and adversity (Deuteronomy 30:15)."

The life choice is to obey the commandments that God gave them in the desert. To choose otherwise is to choose death. And so a few verses later Moses repeated, "I call heaven and earth to witness against you today that I have set before you life and death, blessings and curses. Choose life so that you and your descendants may live, loving the Lord your God, obeying him, and holding fast to him... (Deuteronomy 30:19-20)."

A generation later Joshua in *his* farewell speech to the people he led into the promised land, Joshua seems to offer the people only two choices, when in fact he is offering a third choice that is life-giving.

Having reminded them of their history with God, and of all God has done for them and with them, Joshua said, "Now if you are unwilling to serve the Lord, choose this day whom you will serve, whether the gods your ancestors served in the region beyond the river or the gods of the Amorites in whose land you are living...."

Then, surprise, Joshua introduces a third option, which turns out to be the only option. "…but as for me and my household, we will serve the Lord (Joshua 24:15)."

Historically, there developed within both Judaism and early Christianity something we refer to as "the two ways." The early Christian church manual known as the Didache, or the teaching, begins with these words: "There are two ways, one of life and one of death, and there is a great difference between the two ways." The way of life includes the famous two greatest commandments selected by Jesus (love God and neighbor) as well as the golden rule, as well as both the commandments given to Moses on Mount Sinai and the words of Jesus during the Sermon on the Mount, mixed together in no particular order.

Little known fact — Joshua and Jesus are the same name — Yeshua, which means "he saves," he rescues," and "he delivers." One comes to us through Hebrew to English and one comes from the Hebrew through the Greek to the English.

I bring this up because Jesus seemed to be doing the same thing as Joshua: going beyond two choices to the true life giving choice. In this case the life giving choice isn't simply to obey the commandments or else to disobey them, but to hear Jesus and respond with a higher level of commitment. His commentary on these laws from the Torah, the way, created a better quality of life not only for ourselves, but for all. He would quote from scripture by beginning, "You have heard that it was said to those of ancient times –" but Jesus will take this further.

First, Jesus quoted from one of the Ten Commandments — "You shall not murder" — which I think we can all agree is a good thing! Jesus went further. Not only may you not kill someone, but in a society built on the concept of honor and shame, Jesus took away carrying a grudge, insulting the person you are angry with, being angry at all, and name calling. You may not be literally killing someone, but you are taking away something that gives life — a person's self-respect, their self-esteem.

Some of us, when we were children and complained that about a schoolmate or sibling's name calling, were told, "Sticks and stones may break my bones, but words will never hurt me."

Not true. Words can leave lasting wounds that never heal, and change our perspective of ourselves. To think otherwise, Jesus says, is to risk our relationship with God.

Some might think that by attending worship, giving our offering, and obeying the law about literal murder all will be well, but the threats of Gehenna, referring to the ever-burning trash dump outside of Jerusalem, threats of prison, and most of all the command to leave our offerings at the altar and seek reconciliation with those we have insulted and offended make it clear that we cannot have a good relationship with God and treat each other like dirt.

Nor can we wait until the other person comes to us to complain — the responsibility for reconciliation rests with all of us who know there is a problem. This rejection of anger, and insistence that we can be right with God and wrong with others is unique to Jesus.

Again, when Jesus quoted the commandment against adultery and then equated lust with adultery he pushed a step further, to challenge us on our attitudes. To look on someone with lust may not harm them physically, but any time we turn someone into an object we take away some of what makes them a person. When Jesus expanded upon the punishment, he used what is known as hyperbole, or exaggeration, as a means to getting his point across. One should not actually cut off your right hand, or anything else, because you are striking at the image of God. Each of us bears that image, and even if we are struggling with sin, we need to honor that image.

At the heart of both anger and lust, two very different sins, is that key concept, doing damage to the image of God.

I want to be careful addressing these few words about divorce, especially because so many people use these as "clobber verses," attempting to force people to remain in toxic relationships with individuals who may be damaging the image of God in their spouse and using these verses as a way to legitimize their continued abuse of another. This was a little clearer in Mark's gospel, where Jesus was addressing the misinterpretation by religious authorities of Deuteronomy 24:1-5. One reason next to nothing was said about divorce in the scriptures was that, like weddings, God's people already had customs and laws set up to take care of divorce. Papyrus documents that survived in the dry climate of Egypt have survived to show that Jewish society was careful, once divorce became necessary, to protect the property rights of women who may have been abused. In Deuteronomy, the phrase "but she does not please him because he finds something objectionable about her" leading to a certificate of divorce, involved a verse that referred to an act of public obscenity bordering on insanity. It was followed by a law that exempted men from military service for a year after marriage, which may have led some men to adopt serial divorce and marriage or remarriage as a ploy to get out of that military service.

This was what Jesus was really talking about: religious "experts" reinterpreting specific case law to cover all situations so they could do anything they pleased.

How often have you heard someone be very judgmental about the use of vulgar language, yet throw around the God's name as it if were nothing? By God? My God? And combining God with any number of other inappropriate words? Here Jesus seems to be going beyond the commandment against taking the name of God in vain, and get to the heart of making God a co-signer on your actions by swearing an oath in God's name.

To swear by God, or by heaven, that such and such will be done, whether it is good or evil, is to make God a co-signer in that oath, obligated to carry out whatever doom or wealth we may have promised, regardless of God's will. At the very least, that seems a little presumptuous.

Really, what this does is force us to take a very serious view about the spoken word. How often have you heard someone say something hurtful, and then add, "Just kidding"? How often have you made a spoken promise, but defended not following through by saying there was no contract. It doesn't count. The spoken word is very important.

There are those Christians who refuse to take an oath for this reason. They will affirm, rather than swear by God in a court of law. Whether this is something all Christians should consider is a difficult thing, but consider this. During his trial for his life, Matthew told us, "...the high priest said to him, "I put you under oath before the living God, tell us if you are the Messiah, the Son of God' (Matthew 26:63)." Jesus refused to answer that question, instead responding, "'You have said so," and quoting from the book of Daniel.

Between the "Road Less Traveled", the "Two Ways", and "Third Way", it comes to my mind that everyone listening to Jesus in Jan Brueghel the Elder's painting "The Sermon on the Mount," had to travel their own unique path to find Jesus. Look at these faces as I pan around the painting. Some of them almost seem to be there by accident — but they're there. Some must have set out deliberately to find Jesus because they loved him and adored him. Others may have followed a path to this mountain because they had every reason to be suspicious of him, to dislike him, and maybe they meant to discredit him, but the message is getting through. They are weighing his words in their hearts, even as we are.

Others are concerned only for the effect his words have on the crowd. They didn't want trouble. And they probably didn't want people actually following his words.

Look — there's a man who looks footsore, far to the right of the painting. He was traveling his own road. Perhaps he was traveling on business. Maybe someone in his family was sick and he was on the way to help. He was walking purposefully — but now the crowd has caught his attention. He's looking at you. You who follow Jesus. You who have heard these words of life. And he's considering whether he ought to step to the side and learn more for himself. What will you tell this man when he asks you what's going on? What will you say about Jesus when he expresses skepticism that this man has anything to do with his life?

It's not just your choice. It's everyone's choice that's at stake and you play a part in the choice of other people.

Everyone in the painting had climbed a mountain to get this close to Jesus. For some these are the first steps to heaven, a stairway to heaven, if you will.

Perhaps so. We believe people can repent. They can change. Certainly hearts and minds are being changed among those listening to Jesus and his Sermon on the Mount. For the time being we are capable of making that choice between good and evil. But for how long?

There's no question that genetics plays a part in our ability to choose. We are born with certain predilections. And there's no question that environment has also played a part in our ability to choose as well. Certain factors in the way we grew up and how we were treated, affects our ability to choose. But regardless of our DNA and the baggage of our past, we are still endowed with the ability to make this most serious of choices.

The problem is that if we keep making the wrong choices we give ourselves fewer and fewer options, and less time to change that road. We can damage our body by bad choices, and more crucially, we can damage our souls to the point where some choices are almost impossible.

Jesus is always waiting for an opportunity to light our path, to rush in, to save us.

That's why living the Sermon on the Mount is so important. We are strengthening ourselves, working out our spiritual muscles, so that making the good choice, the life giving choice, is not only possible, but it becomes the default setting.

Choose not only *who* you will serve — the Lord — but *how* you will serve. You have a choice. I have a choice. There are two ways. Your choice matters. The choice before us is as serious as a heart attack. It's not a path to the right or the left. It is truly the road less traveled, because it is the Jesus choice.

Amen.

(I talk more specifically about Jesus and divorce a lot more in the sermon "For Men Only?" found in the CSS book *Mark His Word: Cycle B Sermons for Proper 16 Through Thanksgiving*, 2017, pp 55-62.)

Transfiguration Sunday
Matthew 17:1-9

That's Jesus!

If you're a world traveler you ought to know that if you're in London, you're probably being watched.

There are around one million surveillance cameras in the city of London. Wherever you go, whatever you do, whichever bus, tram, or underground car you get into, you're being filmed. Whatever restaurant you enter, or tourist attraction you visit, it's being recorded.

It's all because of crime, terrorism, and safety. Rest assured, if someone commits a crime they're going to be seen. The question is: Will they be caught?

In 2014, there was a sexual predator stalking the London transit system. He was a middle-aged man wearing glasses and a dark coat. He knew he could be filmed, so he hid himself behind an open newspaper to conceal his identity before he would grope whatever woman sat next to him.

He was filmed coming in and out of the vehicles, but despite knowing which train or bus he was taking, they couldn't identify him because he paid cash instead of using a credit card for his fare. Investigators didn't have a name, and couldn't make an arrest.

Fortunately, in addition to all those cameras, London has a special team of investigators called The Dirty Dozen, a special police unit consisting of officers who have the gift of never forgetting a face. They are called Super Recognizers. It doesn't matter if the suspect dyes their hair, shaves off or grows a beard, smiles, frowns, or has no expression at all, these special cops will recognize them anyway.

Since London has more surveillance cameras throughout the city than most any other city in the world, these officers study faces on digital spreadsheets, lineups, and archived footage so they'll be able to spot individuals of interest at or near other crime scenes.

One day one of those investigators, Allison Young, was looking at the footage of this person, when she happened to look out her office window at the commuters rushing out on the nearby transit station and into the street, when she saw the face of someone walking by and shouted, "That's him!"

She *was* right. It was him. Police rushed out of the station and made an arrest. The individual confessed immediately.

That's him! The Dirty Dozen has recognized and identified plenty of terrorists, thieves, vandals, and other criminals.

Unfortunately, there are individuals who are the opposite of Super Recognizers. These people have a condition known as developmental prosopognosia. Those with an advanced case of prosopognosia are unable to recognize a face under any conditions. As far as I can tell, it comes from the Greek words for face and no knowledge. Even if they look at a familiar face, they don't recognize it.

The official description of the condition simply states: "Developmental prosopagnosia is a condition marked by exceptionally poor face recognition ability despite normal vision and absence of brain damage or other cognitive deficits."[1] Those with a less advanced case, and many of us here probably fall into this category without knowing it, recognize people after we've come to know them, but when they are in a situation where they meet a number of new people they are unable to differentiate them, one from another, for some time.

But those who really have the condition fail to recognize their children, their spouses, and other family members.

In today's scripture we read that six days after Jesus told his disciples what he meant to do — die on the cross in obedience to God the Father, locating his ministry within a landscape of suffering and pain, Jesus took three of his disciples up on a high mountain and was transformed, or as we call it, transfigured.

1   Richard Russel, "Super-recognizers: People with Extraordinary Face Recognition Ability", *Psychonomic Bulletin & Review* vol. 16 no.2 (2009), 252-257. https://www.ncbi.nlm.nih.gov/pmc/articles/PMC3904192/

The Greek word is metamorphized. He morphed into something different. You could translate it this way: "And he metamorphed before them, and his face shone like a the sun, and his clothes became white as the light."

In this story the apostles, with regard to two of the individuals described, should be prosopognosiacs, but in this oddest of circumstances they turned out to be Super Recognizers.

When Jesus was transformed, revealing him as he truly was, he was flanked by Moses and Elijah. There was no way they could have known what either of those two individuals looked like, yet Peter, James, and John recognized them!

Sometimes the disciples of Christ had a hard enough time recognizing Jesus, their constant companion. Remember, when Jesus appeared in another mysterious circumstance, walking on water toward the disciples who were on a boat battling a storm, they did not recognize him, but said, "It is a ghost!" (Matthew 14:26). After his resurrection, Mary of Magdala, two disciples on the road to Emmaus, and the apostles on a boat after a fruitless night of fishing, did not at first recognize Jesus.

Imagine if suddenly you happened upon George Washington or Alexander Hamilton. You might recognize them, even though they died hundreds of years ago, because we could compare their faces to their portraits on the bills in our wallets or purses. The ancients could not have turned to any official portraits of Moses or Elijah hanging near the city gates of Jerusalem for confirmation. It's not clear if the statuary displaying some of the ancient rulers intended to portray them accurately or according to some societal ideal, but we can be sure that neither Moses nor Elijah ever posed for a picture, especially because of the commandment against graven images.

This makes me think that there's something about us in our eternal selves, when we are finally who we were always meant to be, that is instantly recognizable. This is an amazing moment.

And like most amazing moments, it didn't last. But that didn't stop the apostles from trying to preserve this moment. Peter blurts out that it is good for the apostles to be there, and perhaps they should build — what? — dwellings, tents, booths?

The Greek word used for the three structures that the apostle Peter suggests be erected to honor Jesus, Moses, and Elijah was *skene*. We derive from it the word "skin," as in animal skins used to make tents, so it also means "tents," as well as the word "scene", a reference to the animals skins that were painted to provide a scenic backdrop for ancient theatricals. This was indeed a dramatic scene, a turning point in the gospels when Jesus was revealed as fully divine and fully human before his death and resurrection. The offer to build three tents was an appropriate way to provide for the comfort of three honored personages. The tents also called to mind what was sometimes referred to as the tabernacle, a word that hides the fact that the Ark of the Covenant and the presence of God were housed in a tent that traveled with the slaves freed from Egypt as they traveled through the desert, even when their sins stretched the journey to forty years. Perhaps these tents were a way of creating historical markers for this amazing event. I also wonder if Peter mentioned the *skene* because he felt like he had to fill the space with talking, even though an awed silence might have been more appropriate.

I think at its heart this was an attempt by Peter to keep the holy in one spot, as if we could return to a certain place and summon God. All that became moot when the heavenly voice spoke and knocked them senseless. That was a way of knocking some sense into them.

The description — and meaning in part — of this extraordinary event is encapsulated in these words from the second letter of Peter:

For we did not follow cleverly devised myths when we made known to you the power and coming of our Lord Jesus Christ, but we had been eyewitnesses of his majesty. For he received honor and glory from God the Father when that voice was conveyed to him by the Majestic Glory, saying, "This is my Son, my Beloved, with whom I am well pleased." We ourselves heard this voice come from heaven, while we were with him on the holy mountain (2 Peter 1:16-18).

One can hardly imagine how shocking, how startling this was — and yet the three apostles could still say: That's him! Glorified, seemingly beyond recognition, Jesus was recognizable.

Later, hanging, bloodied on the cross, Jesus was recognizable to those who loved him.

Later still — Jesus was recognizable as the risen Lord — even if it sometimes took a moment for his good friends to recognize who stood in their midst.

Mary of Magdala, discovering the tomb was empty and certain that someone had stolen the body, did not recognize Jesus at first either. Then she did. Why? Because Jesus spoke her name, and suddenly she was ready to believe.

Most importantly, the two disciples on the road to Emmaus recognized Jesus in the breaking of the bread. I think when we break bread together, whether in communion at church, fellowship with friends and family, or in ministry with total strangers, we will see Jesus, transformed, in each other's faces.

That's Jesus!

Jesus is all around you. Jesus is recognizable is the faces of infants and the posture of children. Jesus is recognizable in the youngest and the oldest among us and everyone in between. Jesus is recognizable in the poor and the rich and the struggling, the abled and disabled, women and men — Look around us right now.

That's Jesus!

When you see an unaccompanied minor who is a refugee, That's him! You see Jesus.

When you see a homeless person muttering to herself, dragging along a cart full of bags and rags and belongings, That's him — you see Jesus.

When you see one of your friends at the grocery store, and you ask if they are okay, and they say they are okay, but you have to wonder from the expression if they are telling the truth — that's him! You see Jesus.

When you see you in the mirror, and you're wondering just where you're going to get the strength to put on your game face and act like everything's normal — that's him! You're Jesus.

Moses himself was transfigured, after a fashion. We're told in Exodus 24:12-18 that "...the appearance of the glory of the Lord was like a devouring fire on the top of the mountain in the sight of the people of Israel (Exodus 24:17)" and that Moses entered into that devouring fire. Moses was transfigured after a fashion following his close encounters with God's presence.

Elijah was transfigured, when the chariot of fire swooped down and scooped him up. It was such an awe-inspiring sight that Elisha hollered out incoherently, "Father! Father! The chariots of Israel and its horsemen!" Aaron Milovic, in his lengthy book on the slim volume known as the *Didache or The Teaching of the Twelve Apostles,* suggested that the prophets who traveled from church to church in the first Christian century were those who had passed through fire themselves — transfigured by economic misfortune and persecution's flames as well. These individuals would travel to a house church and stay only a night or two in order to tell their story. That house church was an island, a group of committed individuals engaged in a shared business, a craft that put food on the table and kept body and soul together. They struggled to afford to extend hospitality to transfigured guests in hopes of being transformed themselves. When we as churches experience transfigured visitors who bring the blast furnace of their experiences in minister, can we say also, "That's Jesus!" When the sufferings of these traveling prophets breathe new life into our spirits can't we say, "That's Jesus!"

Jesus was radically changed in the Transfiguration, but the apostles still recognized him. And if we are radically transformed by Jesus, we will see people with the eyes of Jesus as well and recognize them for who they truly are.

There's a rabbinic story from the Babylonian Talmud that is retold in several versions. For some Jewish denominations certain prayers are to be recited at dawn, but dawn, unlike sunrise, can be difficult to determine, so some students asked their rabbi "How light does it have to be to constitute dawn?" The rabbi turned the question back to the students. They gave various answers. One said, "When I can see two animals in the field and I can tell the cow from the horse." Another said, "When I can tell a fig tree from an olive tree." And a third said, "When I see a person and can tell if that person is a woman or a man."

"No," said the rabbi, "When you can see a person and know that person is your brother or your sister, when you see that person is your friend, then the night is over and the new day has dawned."

The old hymn says, "When we walk with the Lord in the light of his word, what a glory he casts on our way!" (in the public domain). This should change us. This should transform us too, being one of the disciples.

Are we ready to follow Jesus?

Are we ready to obey Jesus?

As we continue our walk together, are we ready to stand by Jesus?

Stand by Jesus, in all the people you see around you here.

Stand by Jesus, in all the people who go unrecognized by an uncaring world.

Stand by Jesus, throughout this season, through opposition and crisis, and wrongful arrest, and torture, and death.

Stand by Jesus — all the way to the resurrection.

And don't be afraid, while the rest of the world scoffs, to say, "That's Jesus!"

See Jesus.

Amen.

The Other Sermon On the Mount

A long time ago, next to a water cooler, far, far, away....

Okay, maybe not a great beginning for another installment in the *Star Wars* franchise, but I am thinking back to a long forgotten era — before the internet, email, social media, streaming — and trolling. In those days you didn't post pictures, articles, and memes on your Facebook® page. When you did was saunter over to the water cooler to steal a minute with your friends at work. While you were there you also took a moment, while the five-gallon jug of water glugged, glugged, glugged, to take a look at the bulletin board.

It was kind of like the internet. You posted information by thumb tacking it up where everyone could see it. It might be a news story, an inspirational thought, a picture of your grandkids, a little poem, or your favorite Bible verse. People would just stand there and look. They might chuckle, or say to someone else, "Have you seen this?"

Then they might make a photocopy and thumbtack it onto another bulletin board so other people could enjoy.

Eventually really good stuff made the rounds until everyone you knew had seen it.

One of the most famous amusing pieces of writing that was passed along from bulletin board to bulletin board was written by a Unitarian pastor named Robert Fulghum for his church newsletter. It was called "Everything I Ever Needed to Know I Learned in Kindergarten." It was short and funny. Fulghum wrote how we learned to make friends in kindergarten. He helped us remember that naps are good for us and everything lives and dies. The things we learned in kindergarten were true: "Share everything, play fair, don't hit people, put things back where you found them, clean up your own mess."

People passed the piece along, often without the author's name attached. And it went viral in an era when the only thing that went viral were viruses.

Although this is a roundabout way of saying that though most Christians would be surprised to hear it, it's also true: "Everything I ever needed to know about the Sermon on the Mount I learned from the Torah."

At least for Jesus.

The Torah, also known as the Law, consists of what we know as the first five books of the Bible: Genesis, Exodus, Leviticus, Numbers, and Deuteronomy. Jesus, speaking the Sermon on the Mount, draws heavily on the Torah, or Law. And though you probably never open your Bible to Leviticus to read for pleasure, Jesus knew Leviticus very well, and quoted it on several occasions

Jesus ends today's reading of the Sermon on the Mount with the phrase, "Be perfect, therefore, as your heavenly Father is perfect (5:48)." This was meant to call to mind the command in Hebrew repeated several times in Leviticus 19 — "You shall be holy, for I the Lord your God am holy."

Well, I know that being perfect sounds impossible, but actually, no matter how you say it, it's not just expected, but it's also doable. The Greek word *teleios,* like the Hebrew word *tamin,* both translated "perfect," really means mature, and complete. When Jesus tells us to be perfect as our Heavenly Father is perfect, he's really saying, "Grow up." You can do this. Make a mature choice.

And who is called to be perfect? Over the centuries some have suggested just the disciples, and by extension only a small minority of the extra faithful, are supposed to love enemies and turn the other cheek. However, in the Sermon on the Mount Jesus clearly means for everyone to seek this perfection by maturing as disciples.

There's a sad scene toward the end of the musical "Fiddler on the Roof." The Jewish villagers of Anatchevka have been told by the Russian authorities that they had three days to evacuate their beloved homes and leave the territory. All were in shock.

Somebody suggested they take up arms and defend themselves. One of the villagers shouted, "An eye for an eye, and a tooth for a tooth," quoting the scriptures. Tevya, the milkman responded, ruefully, "Very good. That way the whole world will be blind and toothless."

Both the villager in the musical and Jesus in the Sermon on the Mount are looking back at Leviticus 24:20 "fracture for fracture, eye for eye, tooth for tooth…"; Exodus 21:23-25 "life for life, eye for eye, tooth for tooth, hand for hand, foot for foot, burn for burn, wound for wound, bruise for stripe;" and Deuteronomy 19: 21 "life for life, eye for eye, tooth for tooth, hand for hand, foot for foot."

That's a pretty formidable witness, but it's important to note this ancient concept of eye for eye, known as the *lex talionis*, or law of retaliation, was meant as a way of *limiting* revenge, of substituting justice and equivalency for an ever-spiraling cycle of violence among rival clans and tribes. The purpose was to limit the punishment so that it fit the crime.

Indeed, as time went by most cultures, including that which Jesus belonged to, assigned various amounts of money so that if one paid the price, the violence could cease without further violence. One need not actually lose an eye, a tooth, or a hand.

Jesus challenged us to limit the cycle of violence even further. Rather than escalating violence until it went out of control, Jesus called upon us to turn the other cheek, go the second mile when forced by authorities to carry a burden a mile, and to give to everyone in need, deserved or not.

It was legal, but humiliating, for a Roman soldier, a member of a foreign occupying army, to force anyone he chose to carry his pack for a mile. In our own constitution, the rarely quoted or even noted Third Amendment spoke to the same sort of humiliation that Americans in colonial times experienced when British authorities forced them to house and feed English soldiers who were part of that occupying army. That Third Amendment states: "No Soldier shall, in time of peace be quartered in any house, without the consent of the owner, nor in time of war, but in a manner to be prescribed by law."

One reason you haven't had to board a soldier in your home is precisely because of these words. But you may have felt forced, or at least obligated, to help someone when their car is stuck in a ditch, or when someone elderly is struggling with their groceries walking across a parking lot. Other are people are watching. You feel like you have to help. Instead of resenting it, Jesus called on us to look at the situation with different eyes.

Think, next time you feel drafted into helping a friend, relative, or total stranger, of what Simon of Cyrene must have felt when he was forced to carry the crossbar for a condemned prisoner who was staggering toward a horrifying death. Think also how, for years afterward, his acceptance of Jesus' cross must have made him at the very least a celebrity among the Christians he knew. The very fact that he was named suggested that people knew who he was, and made it likely that carrying the cross of Christ led him to follow Jesus.

Jesus carried this idea of nonresistance even further. Most people did not have a closetful of clothes. They had an inner garment and an outer garment. Workers who failed to complete assignments might discover their garment had been confiscated. Jesus counseled his listeners to go further and give all, not just the cloak, but to anyone who asked for money, or who wished to borrow.

This was radical behavior. Jesus himself lived it. During his trial and execution, Jesus did not resist when he was struck on the cheek nor when his garment was taken away.

That leads to an even tougher command from Jesus: loving our enemies.

Some preachers, lawmakers, and demagogues call on us to hate, and to respond to hate with hatred. The Jewish law commanded that anyone who came upon their enemy's ox or donkey wandering lost, or in danger, return it to safety. Still, it had to be totally unexpected when Jesus told the crowds to go farther.

In Matthew 22:33-40, Jesus was asked which law was the greatest. Onlookers probably listened up. This was the kind of legal question that was fun to argue about. His questioners, however, had an ulterior motive. No matter what law Jesus picked, they would try to find something deficient in it, so that Jesus didn't measure up.

Jesus responded on his own terms, quoting not one, but two laws that encapsulated the whole law. The first law called upon to love God with all our heart, soul, and strength. Then Jesus said:

And a second is like it: 'You shall love your neighbor as your-self.' On these two commandments hang all the law and the prophets" (Matthew 22:37-40).

Worth remembering is the clause that preceded these famous words: *"You shall not take vengeance or bear a grudge against any of your people"* (19:18). Loving instead of taking vengeance, the whole point of what Jesus was saying in the Sermon on the Mount, is mirrored in Leviticus. The remedy for revenge, we learn, is in releasing grudges and loving everyone. This is reminiscent of what Martin Luther King Jr., said on more than one occasion, that the purpose of nonviolent resistance based on love is that one hoped to save the bigot in the process. When we are at our best this is the Christian response all of us should choose.

But why did Jesus say that we had heard, from of old, that in addition to loving our neighbor, which it clearly said in Leviticus, to also "… hate your enemy" where did this come from? It did not come from scripture. Where did it come from? Possibly it was a popular proverb — and it may have been the default setting for many people.

Yet Jesus challenged us to transcend conventional wisdom for heavenly wisdom, if for no other reason than the fact that God was already letting the sun shine and the rain fall on all, not just the good. It was and is in doing more than expected that we are finally perfected.

The only other possibility was that Jesus could have been speaking about the Dead Sea Scrolls community, a very influential group in his day, who commanded the "sons of light" to hate the "sons of darkness" (Community Rule 1:10-11).

In Jesus' day, many people considered foreigners, resident aliens, those who belonged to another country or another faith, their natural enemies. Leviticus turned that idea upside down when it said:

When an alien resides with you in your land, you shall not oppress the alien. The alien who resides with you shall be to you as the citizen among you; you shall love the alien as yourself, for you were aliens in the land of Egypt: I am the LORD your God (19:33-34).

Some say this is the most radical verse in the Bible, the ethical summit of scripture. It turns our expectations upside down. And it includes one of the other essential ideas of Leviticus 19, that the poor have a right to what is owned by the rich.

When you reap the harvest of your land, you shall not reap to the very edges of your field, or gather the gleanings of your harvest. You shall not strip your vineyard bare, or gather the fallen grapes of your vineyard; you shall leave them for the poor and the alien: I am the LORD your God (19:9-10).

God's safety net, the equivalent of our social services is for both the poor and the alien. This is what it means to love your enemy.

Our faith is a living faith. We are living temples. This is something visible to the world, whether or not you're a believer. The way we conduct ourselves, what we *do*, defines who we are, and also how Christ appears through us to the larger world.

God's command to love is both a call to action as well as feelings.

Hebrew is a concrete language where things happen. There is less abstract thinking, more solidity. This is demonstrated in the Hebrew word (*'āhēb*) translated as love. It means more than warm fuzzies. Love is compassionate deeds.

You are not merely to tolerate the alien in your midst. You are not simply to allow the alien to live among you when it's financially beneficial to you, then kick out the aliens when there is an economic downturn. You are not to fearmonger the populace with rumors about aliens. You are to *love* the alien as yourself.

Just as we Americans are a nation of immigrants, and our ancestors came from somewhere else, so too God reminded the people the reason we do this is because: "…you were aliens in the land of Egypt." Finally the words make it clear that there is no choice regarding this command to love—"I am the Lord your God." That was the Leviticus way of saying what Jesus emphasized — be perfect as your Father in heaven is perfect.

Love the alien. Love your enemy. There is nothing like this in the ancient world. Aliens were necessary as workers and merchants, but they might or might not have rights in the country they lived in. They could often be abused with impunity. Aliens had no recourse. They didn't know the rules, didn't know what was fair, and if they were in a dispute with a native, who would stand up for them? But here God proclaimed they were to be shown positive love. They matter.

Remember, this was a part of a speech delivered to the whole assembly. The purpose was to call the people to holy living, separate living, different living. Loving the alien was an essential part of that... radical.

Jan Brueghel the Elder was Flemish, and many of the people in this painting of "The Sermon on the Mount" were white. That would not have been the case with the people at the real Sermon on the Mount, but that's not important at this moment. Brueghel, like many people, set the gospel story in their own time and place and that's what he's done.

But notice there are a few brown people scattered throughout the crowd. Would they have been people brought over from some of the colonies? Did they travel there? I don't know. But I notice a couple of folks watching the foreigners instead of Jesus. One guy seemed amused. This called to mind the words of Leviticus — "You shall love the alien in your midst as yourselves," as well the words Jesus spoke about loving your enemies. So many people, then as now, were taught to be suspicious of foreigners.

Let's scroll some more around the crowd in this painting, There are figures of authority scattered throughout the scene. Soldiers were carrying pikes. Some were listening to Jesus. Others were looking around the crowd. And there were some figures of authority on horseback. One in a central position with his back to us is looking across the crowd to his right toward another authority figure. What were they thinking? What opinion were they expressing in their gaze? Were they wondering — is this Jesus too radical? Did they want people to stop hating, to start loving, to turn the other cheek?The Hebrew word for love is dangerous, because love is not just a feeling. Love is expressed in action. What if people start loving those designated as the enemy of the month by those in authority?

You have a choice. I have a choice. Our choice matters. it's the adult choice, the mature choice. The only choice. Love your enemies.

Like Jesus.

Amen.

Eighth Sunday after the Epiphany
Matthew 6:24-34

Food, Water, Shelter, Clothing – and Jesus?

The Hitchhiker's Guide to the Galaxy, by Douglas Adams, was a trilogy that consisted of five books. Within its covers you will learn that the actual *Hitchhiker's Guide to the Galaxy* is a book that sells a little better than the *Encyclopedia Galactica* because it costs a little less and had the words "Don't Panic!" on the cover.

The series followed the adventures of Arthur Dent, an earthman who discovered his friend Ford Prefect was actually an alien from outer space who was doing research on our planet so he could write the entry about Earth for the guide. Dent is the only resident of Earth to escape when our planet is destroyed to make room for an intergalactic bypass. At one point the crew decides they're all a little hungry, which brings up the following information from the *Hitchhiker's Guide*:

The History of every major Galactic Civilization tends to pass through three distinct and recognizable phases, those of Survival, Inquiry and Sophistication, otherwise known as the How, Why, and Where phases. For instance, the first phase is characterized by the question 'How can we eat?' the second by the question 'Why do we eat?' and the third by the question 'Where shall we have lunch?"

As it turned out, they ended up at the restaurant at the end of the universe, which refers not to the physical edge of the universe, but the chronological end. The restaurant was located at the end of time.

In this passage, Douglas Adams was making fun of the list of basic needs that every person thinks they need, compared with what we really need, for survival: food, water, shelter, and clothing. After a natural disaster, even in a first world developed country like our own, these were the needs that disaster relief agencies worked to provide, in order to help totally displaced and disoriented people begin to make sense of the world. Often these folks have lost everything without any warnings. Everything they owned had been destroyed, and with it any sense of safety and security.

Before we can think about faith, hope, and the meaning of life, these need to be provided.

Let me emphasize, people recovering from a disaster are *not* the people Jesus addressed in the Sermon on the Mount, when he said these words: "Therefore I tell you, do not worry about your life, what you will eat or what you will drink, or about your body, what you will wear. Is not life more than food, and the body more than clothing?" Those desperately down and out can think of nothing but food, drink, holding body and soul together, and clothes.

As it is, the people Jesus addressed were desperate enough, many of them living from day to day, unsure of if or when they would work again. We met shepherds watching their flocks by night, only these were probably not their sheep, but belong to another. Those were tough times.

Indeed most times were tough times. The stories told by the ancients often centered around the great difficulty of human existence. The Sumerian story of Gilgamesh, a great hunter and warrior, the greatest her of all time, centers on the death of his close friend and the deep sorrow this causes him. Gilgamesh sets out on a great quest to bring back a plant that will restore life to his friend and grant eternal life — but though he succeeds in finding and taking hold of the plant, he fails to hold on to it. Mortality reigns.

In Greek mythology, anxiety was seen as a destructive force that afflicts all humankind. The poet Hesiod wrote about an age of gold in which humanity was free from care, but when Pandora took the lid off the jar sorrow is loosed on the world.

There were portions of the Hebrew Bible, like Ecclesiastes and Job, which shared some of this anxiety about our condition. We were sent naked and helpless into the word. Dust we are, and to dust we shall return.

As the Wisdom book Sirach, a part of the apocrypha, puts it: "Jealousy and anger shorten life, and anxiety brings on premature old age" (Sirach 30:24).

When you come right down to it, the Beatitudes, part of the Sermon on the Mount, listed very real daily troubles. Poverty, sorrow, brutality, injustice, lack of mercy, impure hearts, war, persecution, and martyrdom.

So how can you tell us, Jesus, "Do not worry! No exceptions!?" We are engaged in worry from dawn to dusk in an uncertain world where huge chunks of money in our pension plans can disappear in a heartbeat, and our heartbeat can suddenly disappear as well!

I'm reminded of a passage from the Hebrew scriptures. The prophet Habakkuk complains to God because there's so much injustice! God replied in effect "I've got this covered. I'm sending the Babylonians who chew up nations for lunch and spit them out. They'll destroy all of you." Habakkuk protests — "What kind of answer is that? You're immortal. We're not." And God replied, "The righteous will live by their faith."

I'm not sure how satisfying God's answer was there, and in this passage, at first glance, I'm puzzled by the answer of Jesus.

Jesus gave two sets of proof to back up his demand that we not worry.

The first compared animals and humans, using the birds as examples. In this case, Jesus pointed to the tasks given to men in that society — "…they neither sow nor reap nor gather into bards, and yet our heavenly Father feeds them. Aren't you worth more than they?"

The second example compared humans to plants. "Consider the lilies of the field, how they grow; they neither toil nor spin, yet I tell you, even Solomon in all his glory was not clothed like one of these." In this instance, Jesus alluded to some of the tasks assigned to women in that culture. This is how Jesus emphasized worry and anxiety was common to both women and men. With this example Jesus was lampooning the fashions of the royal court, where great attention was paid to colors, to precious stones, to symbols of wealth equally symbols of power.

Aren't lilies in all their simplicity more beautiful than humans bedecked in garish but meaningless displays?

One may answer that the lilies of the field, like all flowers, bloom, wither, and die. But in their brief flowering they point to their creator, who is greater and eternal. They point to God's expectations for all of us. I think that's why Julia Ward Howe used the image of lilies in her immortal "Battle Hymn of the Republic," where the lilies are compared to the brief but immortal ministry of Jesus:

> *In the beauty of the lilies Christ was born across the sea,*
> *With a glory in His bosom that transfigures you and me.*
> *As He died to make men holy, let us die to make men free,*
> *While God is marching on.* (In the public domain.)

The brevity of glory is emphasized with the next example drawn from the world of plants — the beauty with which God clothes the ordinary grasses, which are "alive today and tomorrow thrown into the oven...."

But Jesus, who knows Isaiah's words —

> *A voice says, "Cry out!"*
> *And I said, "What shall I cry?"*
> *All people are grass,*
> *their constancy is like the flower of the field.*
> *The grass withers, the flower fades*
> *when the breath of the Lord blows upon it;*
> *surely the people are grass.*
> *The grass withers, the flower fades;*
> *but the word of our God will stand forever"*
> (Isaiah 40:6-7).

— tells us to hitch our wagon to the star of God's word: "But strive first for the kingdom of God and his righteousness, and all these things will be given to you as well" (6:33). Do not do as the nations do, striving constantly for the things of this earth that are transient as us!

When Jesus asks us to consider birds, animals, and all life with whom we share this globe, I think he's saying something very important.

It's not all about us.

When you think about it, this was God's answer to Job too! Job had a legitimate case in that lengthy book. Job knew nothing of the verbal sparring between God and the adversary, who in that book seems to be a member of the heavenly court whose job is like a prosecuting attorney — make the case against the plaintiff before the divine judge. All he knew was that he had lost his children, his possessions, and his health, and he didn't do anything to deserve it. Job complained that he didn't deserve his fate and lamented that he couldn't get a fair hearing in an impartial court. He wanted to hear God's answer — and God answered — without directly addressing Job's accusations.

Instead, God told Job to pull up his big-boy underwear — kind of — that's what girding his loins means — tightening his belt to prepare for battle, and then God showed Job the universe. It was, and is, a big universe. Anyone who has seen photographs like the Pillars of Creation taken by the Hubble Telescope has glimpsed that they can't grasp the immensity of God's universe. And the more we know about the animals and plant life we share this small blue dot with, the greater our awe.

God in effect told Job that it was not all about him, but that he was a part of this great creation, he could handle the immensity of all, and he had a right to be there too.

The big picture is crucial to our understanding of how much of God's good earth we don't understand. That brings me back to the painting "The Sermon on the Mount," by Jan Brueghel the Elder. Let's take a look again. At the right hand edge of the crowd were some well-dressed folks arriving from the city. There was some money there. But a man dressed in the more plain garb of a scholar was pointing them to Jesus. Let's pan back until we see the whole picture. Jesus was a small figure, almost lost. Indeed, all those people, each one a painstakingly painted representation of a human being, including Jesus, almost shrink to insignificance. The crowd listening or ignoring the Sermon on the Mount take up less than a third of the painting! Look at the trees. Aren't they glorious? Let's zoom in — look at how the artist has given as much attention to individual leaves as to individual faces! Was that necessary? I think it was. The natural world that we share on this globe is precious to God as much as we are. Let's gaze at the trees. You could see that one bird up to the right soaring above the city far below, almost lost in the haze. And look at the birds resting on the branches or on the trunk of a tree! That's not to mention the dogs and horses we find scattered throughout this painting.

What it comes down to is the truth of the statement made by Jesus at the beginning of today's reading: "No one can serve two masters. ….You cannot serve God and mammon" (6:24).

Perspective.

At the start of our recent pandemic much was made of using the time wisely, reminding people that Shakespeare wrote his play "King Lear," during one outbreak of the plague that closed the theaters. In that play King Lear decided to retire and divide his kingdom between his three daughters, planning to live with each one in turn. All he wanted was for them to say how much they loved him. Two of the daughters, both married, insisted they loved no one more than their father, trying to outdo the other in their sickening flattery. The third daughter, Cordelia, reminded her father that when she got married she must put her new family before him even as she continued to love him. Enraged, her father cursed her and banished her from his sight, dividing her third of the kingdom between her two sisters.

The irony is that the first two daughters loved themselves more than their father, mocking him once the kingdom was theirs and casting him out homeless into the storm. The third daughter, who had her priorities straight died alongside her father fighting to put him back on his rightful throne.

The Aramaic word *mammon* is the false god of wealth and property, here personified as a master. We will either be a slave of mammon or a slave of God. The ancients recognized that mammon was not a real god, in the sense of one of the man gods worshiped by believers. It is a non-existent god. One who serves mammon serves nothing.

When we are able to use money, which is not intrinsically evil, for as the Apostle Paul noted, "For the love of money" not the money itself "is the root of all kinds of evil" (1 Timothy 6:10), then we are prioritizing the world correctly. Serve God. Avoid the trap of materialism, which is not a god. It is nothing.

The rich young man in Mark 10:17-22 pleased Jesus with his knowledge of the commandments and his commitment to living them, but it grieved Jesus when he was unable to separate himself from his wealth. The non-existent god mammon was too powerful. Compare that to the gratitude of Mary of Magdala, beset with the demons of depression and mental illness, and liberated from them by Jesus, followed Jesus, and with her money supported his ministries (Luke 8:1-3).

Perspective — get a perspective to see our place in the great universe, and our place in the heart of Jesus as well. "Are you not of more value than they?" Jesus asked, referring both to the birds of the air and the lilies of the field. Our Father knows our needs.

Perspective — begin to pray for neither too much nor too little, but just enough. As Agur prayed in Proverbs 30:7-9

> *Two things I ask of you;*
> *do not deny them to me before I die:*
> *Remove far from me falsehood and lying;*
> *give me neither poverty nor riches;*
> *feed me with the food that I need,*
> *or I shall be full, and deny you,*
> *and say, "Who is the Lord?"*
> *or I shall be poor, and steal,*
> *and profane the name of my God.*

Come to think of it, Jesus said the same thing when he said "Give us this day our daily bread (Matthew 6:11)." Consider the lilies of the field. Consider the birds of the air. Give me enough, Lord, but not so much that I think I don't need you. Help me remember just how much I depend on you, and how much you love me!

Amen.

I Never Knew You!

A friend told me his kids were very particular when it came to which version of a classic story was read to them. For instance, his kids demanded what he called "the King James Version" of "The Three Little Pigs."

The story, which made its first printed appearance less than two hundred years ago, may well be much older. Three pigs, all brothers, were sent out by their mother to make their fortunes. The first came across a man with a load of hay and, having asked for and been given the hay, built a house out of it. The second pig came upon a man with a load of wood, with the same result.

The third pig acted more wisely and builds his home out of bricks. Some versions strengthen this point by showing the first two pigs at play, having built their flimsy homes quickly, while the third brother pig was slaving away.

Along came the Big, Bad Wolf, who, having been refused entrance in turn at each of the homes of the three pigs, huffed and puffed to blow their houses down. This worked for the first two pigs, but no amount of huffing and puffing had any effect on the house of bricks.

In most modern versions the first two pigs ran off in fear of the wolf after their homes were blown down, ultimately ending up at the brick house of the third pig. The wolf failed to blow that house down.

All three pigs were saved!

But my friend's kids wanted the more realistic old fashioned King James version, where pigs one and two were eaten by the big bad wolf after he blew down their houses. The wolf himself, having climbed down the chimney of the brick house, died in the third pig's stewpot.

I'm not sure why they preferred that version, but I will say there's a stark contrast between the consequences for the foolish pigs and the Big, Bad Wolf.

That stark contrast is at the heart of this final look at the Sermon on the Mount in the gospel of Matthew. Jesus made it clear — those who not only heard his words but also acted on them were like the wise pig — whoops — the wise man who built his house on rock versus the foolish man who built his house on sand.

Like any good children's story, there is parallel language for the two different examples, which makes the contrast all the greater when Jesus concludes his story by saying "The rain fell, the floods came, and the winds blew and beat on that house –" to emphasize the contrast between the wise and foolish man. Jesus was describing weather patterns known only too well by his listeners, as his parables tended to be grounded in day to day reality. The images were violent, because disaster can strike swiftly. In the hot, dry world of the Middle East storms come quickly without any warning, and dry riverbeds, called *wadis*, can suddenly become channels for rushing floods, scouring everything in their paths.

Even though we know this to be true, houses can be quickly built on sand and seem secure, only to be washed away without warning when the storms batter and pound the landscape. Alas, the fate of the one who builds a house with shoddy equipment can be the same as the foolish pigs.

The wise man's house stood, despite the violent weather. The word for "wise," *phronius*, implies wisdom that comes from using your brain, thinking it through, relying on your intelligence. And Jesus was using the image of a well-built house to personify the kind of smarts that went with not only hearing his words, but also acting on them — living them. It's not enough to know you should build a house out of bricks if you live around wolves, or a house on rock if you live in a stormy environment. You have to actually do it!

We can know something in our head and still make bad choices. I love how Jesus ended his story about the house build on sand — "…and it fell — and great was its fall!"

Which calls to mind, shades of the house built on sand and the foolish pigs, one stark example. On December 14, 1963, the Baldwin Hills Dam, overlooking a densely populated residential area of the Los Angeles basin, showed signs of cracking. Finished only twelve years earlier, its builder ignored the reports of the civil engineers who insisted that building on an earthquake fault line could lead to a disaster similar to the St. Francis Dam in 1928 that had killed over four hundred people.

When the Baldwin Hills Dam finally cracked, then broke, it spilled 225 million gallons, destroying 227 homes. Fortunately only five lives were lost, largely because a local news station covered the impending disaster live, using their new helicopters. People saw the coverage and that, combined with rescue crews sent in advance to evacuate the region, cut down on the magnitude of the disaster. Still, great was its fall — a fall that could have been avoided with some smarts.

The "Prudent Man" was a stock character in the ancient world. That Prudent Man might be annoyingly right on occasion — but he was right. Both the Greek speaking world and the Hebrew world shared this idea of the prudent or wise man, the person who combined both theory and practice was one who had wisdom and understanding.

This is the person who built their house on rock, the pig who built a house of brick, the designer who actually looked over the map for fault lines — that's an important person. And it ought to be us.

Jesus wants it to be us when it comes to both hearing and acting on his words. Living the life of a disciple of Jesus, not just someone who can throw around a verse or two at the right moment, is like building a house wisely. This passage comes at the end of the Sermon on the Mount, this greatest collection of his sayings that are challenging, but also life-giving. We've turned the other cheek, considered the lilies of the field, carried a pack for an extra mile, and struggled to love our enemies — and there's a good reason why.

I've deliberately spoken to the second part of the passage first. Now it's time to get to the first part last.

Jesus begins, "Not everyone who says to me 'Lord, Lord,' will enter the kingdom of heaven, but only the one who does the will of my Father in heaven." Typically in the ancient world the emperors, generals, and other officials required flattery when they arrived in a town. Yet the flatterer was not considered admirable in the ancient world any more than now. The ancient writer Theophrastus (370-285 BC) wrote a work called "The Characters," in which he painted pictures in words about, among many others, the Flatterer. If someone rich or important "made a tasteless joke, he laughed at it and pushed his cloak into his mouth to show he couldn't contain his laughter. …He said that his house had been well laid out, his farm we cultivated, and his portrait a perfect resemblance." In short, "…the flatterer was on the lookout for everything in word or deed by which he thought he would curry favor."

But Jesus didn't need flatterers. Calling out "Lord, Lord" doesn't impress God.

Calling out "Lord, Lord," in a mistaken idea that salvation by faith means mumbling the right words to save yourself from hell is not enough, either. I am reminded of the words of the prophets that honoring God with rituals and words is not enough.

"For I desire steadfast love and not sacrifice, the knowledge of God rather than burnt offerings," Hosea said (Hosea 6:6).

Or Isaiah: "What to me is the multitude of your sacrifices? Says the Lord. I have had enough of burnt offerings of rams and the fat of fed beasts; I do not delight in the blood of bulls, or of lambs, or of goats" (1:11).

When God through Hosea called for steadfast love, he was not talking about feelings — *love*, a word that in Hebrew sounds like the beating of a heart, is not just a feeling — it's action. Like Eliza Doolittle impatiently sings in the musical *My Fair Lady*, "Don't *talk* of love — show me!"

Some may wonder what this meant when the Apostle Paul spoke of salvation by faith, calling to mind what the prophet Joel said — "Then everyone who calls on the name of the Lord will be saved" (Joel 3:23). Certainly Paul had this in mind when he said in Romans 10:8: "For if you confess with your mouth 'Jesus is Lord' and believe in your heart that God raised him from the dead, you will be saved." But Paul, having been taught biblical interpretation by the great teacher Gamaliel, who was in turn taught by one some of the ancient rabbis considered the greatest teacher of all, Hillel, would have understood that God's word calls for action.

Hillel, who died in the year 10 AD at the ripe old age of 110, was once challenged to recite the whole of the Law while standing on one leg. He replied with one of the two versions of the Golden Rule: "Whatever you don't want done to you, don't do to another!"

Typically in the ancient world the emperors, generals, and other officials required flattery when they arrived in a town. But Jesus wanted none of this. Calling out "Lord, Lord," would not suffice.

Faith and works are two sides of the same coin. Paul knew that from his Jewish upbringing. Calling upon the name of the Lord has to lead to adoption of the words of Jesus.

This is dead serious. Jesus uses end time language when he says, simply, "Oh that day...." In the prophetic age, the prophets warned the people not to think the Day of the Lord, when it came, would necessarily be good news. "Alas for you who desire the day of the Lord!" Amos proclaimed. "Why do you want the day of the Lord? It is darkness, not light" (Amos 5:18).

Jesus knew that some would protest, "Lord, Lord," repeating that term of flattery, "did we not prophesy in your name, and cast our demons in your name, and do many deeds of power in your name?" (7:22). But this Sermon on the Mount calls us to become more than believers. We are called to be disciples, partners in healing, sharers in a great hope. It's not enough to avoid doing physical harm to others — anger against others can destroy us from within. Committing adultery in our hearts, swearing in the name of the Lord and in the process making God an involuntary cosigner to our own politics and business practices, practicing our piety in public instead of living lives of true discipleship — this is what it means to *not* be a follower of Jesus.

Can you imagine what it would be like to be complacent, certain that your faith is fire insurance, sitting on the sidelines, until that day when Jesus says, "I never knew you..."?

Interestingly enough, the response of "the crowds" to these strong words by Jesus was not rejection, as would so often happen in the gospels from people in authority and power, but astonishment. As Matthew noted, this Galilean "taught them as one having authority, and not as their scribes." Not like their so-called biblical experts.

If nothing else, this should help us settle the matter posed by some over the centuries who insisted that the Sermon on the Mount was delivered only to the apostles, and therefore was meant only for clergy, or for those separating themselves from the world, and not for rulers, the rich and powerful, or even ordinary folks in the pew. While Jesus may have called his disciples to himself at the beginning of the Sermon on the Mount, the crowds who had been looking for him had followed, and they were not only listening, but were impressed. The Sermon on the Mount is for all of us, after all. It is for all of us who would be disciples of Jesus. And we know this in our heart of hearts.

Let's take a look for a last time at Jan Breughel's extraordinary painting of "The Sermon on the Mount." There's a little group in the far lower left hand corner, listening to another, perhaps self-proclaimed expert, who is drawing their attention away from Jesus. This figure, whose back we see, is dressed in brown, and gesturing with authority. The others, looking pretty well off, and self-satisfied, are smiling, hearing something they want to hear. Perhaps this figure is telling them not to worry about trying to measure up.

Now let us go back to Jesus. He and some of those who surrounded him who may be his apostles, were dressed in what I would call "biblical" costumes, like robes, unlike most of the listeners who are wearing "modern day" clothes, modern day in the sense of what Jan Brueghel's contemporaries would have worn. The artist is putting us in the picture. We are there, also. When we listen to Jesus from a distance of 2,000 years, we are listening to him today, right now.

Look at those faces. I see some sadness. Perhaps some of these people are reflecting on what they've done in the past, and what they need to change. I see some smiles. I see attention wandering on a few faces. Maybe some anger. Not everyone likes the good news of the kingdom, not if it's going to cost them money, status, or power.

Most of all I see light — the light of Jesus Christ, the man of sorrows, telling us honestly what it means to have faith in him, and how we should, here at the end of this sermon, build a firm foundation on the solid rock of his teachings. Listen and do. You have the tools. You have the talent. Go and do thou likewise.

Be wise. Build on the firm foundation. And like this wonderful little painting, keep Jesus at the center. His words are audacious, life giving, astounding, challenging, and essential.

Amen.

www.ingramcontent.com/pod-product-compliance
Lightning Source LLC
Chambersburg PA
CBHW021333090426
42742CB00008B/585